Log Homes Made Easy™

Project Planner

Log Homes Made Easy™
Project Planner

Jim Cooper

First Edition

Log Home Books
Jefferson City, Missouri
2001

Log Homes Made Easy™
Project Planner

By Jim Cooper

Published by:
Log Home Books
PO Box 169
Eureka, MO 63051 U.S.A.

Copyright © 2001
by Jim Cooper
First Printing 2001
Printed in the United States of America

10 9 8 7 6 5 4 3 2

Publisher's Cataloging-In-Publication
(provided by Quality Books, Inc.)

Cooper, Jim, 1949-
   Log home project planner / Jim Cooper. — 1st ed.
   p. cm.
   ISBN: 0-9708055-0-0

   1. Log cabins--Design and construction—Amateurs' manuals. 2. House construction—Amateurs' manuals. I. Title.

TH4840.C66 2001   690'.837
           QBI01-200291

Table of Contents

About the Author

Jim Cooper's involvement in log homes spans more than 15 years. He has been a log home general contractor, builder and construction consultant, sales and marketing vice-president for a major log home company and a writer/photographer on the topic of log homes and log home construction. As a builder, his first log home project won an Award for Excellence from the local chapter of the National Association of Home Builders. The home was featured in the April-May 1990 issue of *Log Home Living*. In 1998, his book Log Homes Made Easy: Contracting and Building Your Own Log Home was the top-selling book in the home planning category at Amazon.com. His column "Brass Tacks" has appeared regularly in *Log Home Living* magazine since 1992. His articles and photographs have also appeared in *Log Homes Illustrated*, *Country's Best Log Homes* and *Log Home Design Ideas*. He has also spoken and written about log homes for the Log Homes Council of the National Association of Homebuilders and authored the Log Homes Council publication *Appraising Log Homes.* In addition to acting as a construction consultant on log projects, Jim currently conducts workshops on *How To General Contract Your Own Log Home* and other log home-related topics. He is also President of Three Creeks Interactive, Inc., developer of Log Home Plans Online (www.loghomeplansonline.com) and Log Homes Made Easy Online (www.easyloghome.com), and is currently developing other online tools to assist log home purchasers and owners. Jim lives in Missouri with his wife, Cheryl, and their two cats Buster and Boo.

Acknowledgments

The *Log Home Project Planner* is the result of years of experience building log homes as well as the accumulated suggestions from many people who have used the tips and forms from my book, <u>Log Homes Made Easy</u>. I wish to thank the many subcontractors, suppliers and building inspectors and owner-contractors and builders who contributed their advice and input.

As with my other log home projects, the *Project Planner* has been a family effort. I want to especially thank my wife, Cheryl who dug into her jounalism background to lay out and proof the manuscript and to my parents who also contributed suggestions and valuable proofreading support.

Finally, I want to thank the many people who have used <u>Log Homes Made Easy</u> in their own log home projects and have shared their experiences with me. Your input has made the *Log Home Project Planner* a better and more thorough book.

The *Log Home Project Planner* is dedicated to the intrepid souls who want to tackle managing or constructing their own log home. In a world where the challenges to homeowner-contractors are substantial, I salute you.

Best wishes for your own log home dream!

--Jim Cooper

Disclaimer

The *Log Home Project Planner* is based on professional experience in general contracting and constructing log homes. Every precaution has been taken in preparing the *Log Home Project Planner* to help you have a safe and successful construction experience. However, neither Log Home Books nor the author assume any responsibility for damages, costs or injury incurred while constructing your home.

Instructions, suggestions and methods suggested in the *Log Home Project Planner* are not intended to replace or supercede the construction manual, blueprints or materials lists prepared by your log provider. It is very important to follow construction methods and instructions in your log provider's construction manual. Failure to do so can lead to later problems and void any warranty protection. Use the *Log Home Project Planner* to supplement any blueprints, materials lists and manuals provided by your architect or log provider.

How To Use The Project Planner

Welcome to the Log Home Project Planner

The *Log Home Project Planner* is about building a log home. It isn't intended to cover designing your home (although you can use the cost estimating system to see the effect of various design features), choosing a log company or purchasing a log package. Those are covered in detail in my book <u>Log Homes Made Easy</u>. For our purposes in this workbook, we'll assume that you have at least preliminary floor plans and elevation drawings for your log home and an estimate of the log package cost from a log provider (either a manufacturer or handcrafter). You also should have a list of the items that are included in the log package or "kit". This list should name specific items, although the package provider won't include exact quantities until your blueprints are complete. If you have completed blueprints and an exact materials list, your estimating accuracy will improve.

You'll use the *Project Planner* to obtain accurate bids from which you can determine an accurate cost for your project, select subcontractors and suppliers and evaluate the impact of choices you make, schedule work and manage your construction project. The *Project Planner* assumes that you have little prior experience with managing a large construction project. The worksheets are designed to accommodate work that will be done by subcontractors as well as labor and materials you intend to provide. While the *Project Planner* was written for log home projects, it works perfectly well for timber frame projects too. Simply substitute "timber frame" where you read "log home". This is possible because, while you may use different suppliers or subcontractors in different types of construction, the process remains the same. Minor differences in sequence will be pointed out in the introduction to each of the Project Planner Sections.

This workbook is meant to be abused. When you are through with it, the pages should be covered with margin notes, cross-outs, calculations and coffee-stains. They should be dog-eared and worn and most important, your *Planner* should be sitting on a shelf in your log home along with a scrapbook full of construction pictures. If you've diligently used the forms and followed the *Planner* sequence, the log home you move into should cost significantly less than had you used the "Just go for it, it'll cost what it costs" approach explained to me by individuals who discovered too late the costs of lack of organization.

Acting as your own General Contractor

There is good news and bad news about acting as your own general contractor in a log home project (or any kind of home-building project). The good news is that you can save a significant amount of money and you don't have to be an experienced construction professional (although it certainly helps). The bad news is that lack of organization or poor management of a construction process can result in a home costing substantially more than if you hired a professional general contractor (GC). I'm not talking a few hundred or thousand dollars here, but tens of thousands. The main causes of cost overruns in a construction project are 1) inaccurate or incomplete specifications that lead to inaccurate bids, 2) poor selection of subcontractors, 3) poor management of the construction process. Of these three, only the first is helped significantly by a detailed understanding of construction and the *Planner* is designed to help you compensate for the experience you may not have. The other two involve mainly the personality and time commitment of the person(s) acting as GC. If you think you can hire a bunch of subcontractors, give them a set of blueprints and show up a couple of times a week to see how things are going, you'd best set this book back on the shelf and put the money toward hiring a real GC.

General contracting requires good organizational skills, attention to detail and a substantial time commitment. It also requires a personality that can stand up to attitudes that occasionally show up on job sites among people who are often paid too little to do hot, hard, dirty, dangerous work or are simply in the business because there are often few entrance requirements. Notice that the skills I listed for general contracting did not include professional construction experience. In fact, I've worked with many people and met many more who, with no construction background, general contracted their own log home, saved money, and had fun. A few had so much fun they either repeated the experience for themselves or a friend or turned it into a business.

How the Project Planner is Organized

The *Project Planner* is organized into five main sections: **Requests for Quotation**, **Cost Estimating Worksheets**, **Supporting Worksheets and Schedules**, **Construction Calendar** and **Miscellaneous Forms**. These appear in the approximate order that you will encounter them in your project. Where the sequence deviates from normal project flow, you'll be directed to the appropriate pages.

The *Project Planner* follows a sequence common to any home construction project:

- Prepare a design (blueprints) and preliminary specifications
- Obtain accurate bids (Requests for Quotation and Supporting Worksheets and Schedules)
- Prepare detailed cost estimate or budget (Cost Estimating)
- Build (Construction Calendar and Miscellaneous Forms)

Your project will be much simplified if you follow this sequence exactly. Waiting until you've started construction to obtain bids for certain things can lead to some nasty surprises. Within each step of the sequence are important sub-steps. For example, to prepare a detailed cost estimate in Section II of the *Planner*, you will have to select bids from among those gathered using the Requests for Quotations in Section I. Instructions for preparing Requests for Quotations and finding subcontractors and suppliers appear at the beginning of Section I. Instructions for evaluating bids and choosing subcontractors appear at the beginning of Section II.

Each section of the Planner begins with a brief explanation of the section's forms and worksheets and the role they play in the overall construction process. Specific instructions, tips or explanations appear on the individual worksheet.

Preparing Your Planner

If you are in the preliminary planning stages, you may prefer to keep the *Planner* intact and fill in the workbook using a soft (easily erased) pencil. When the time comes to get serious, however, I suggest you take the *Planner* apart, three-hole punch the pages and place them into a notebook. There are several reasons for this. You will often require multiple copies of a form. (The forms have been designed with this in mind). Having them loose will make copying easier. Also, a notebook offers better protection on jobsites and riding around in your car or truck (which is where the *Planner* should be during construction.) You may prefer to work only with copies of the *Planner* pages, keeping the originals as masters. I encourage this. I ask only that you respect the copyright notice and copy only for your own use. Since I rely on income from the *Planner* to be able to continue to write and teach about building log homes, I ask you not to share your *Project Planner* with others. There is an order form at the back of the book if you have interested friends or family.

TIP!

> *To separate your Planner pages for copying, take them to a copy center or printer such as Kinko's. Ask them to three-hole punch the Planner and chop off the binding. Look for a notebook that contains pockets to keep loose papers such as subcontractors bids or receipts. Section dividers that also have storage pockets are available from any large office supply store.*

Computers and the Project Planner

At this point, the question inevitably appears, "Is this available on computer". In fact, it may be. As this goes to press, I'm working on a downloadable version that will be available on my website *www.easyloghome.com*. If you would prefer an electronic version, look there. However, I want to offer a word of warning: The "old" saying, "To err is human, to really screw things up requires a computer" was coined for the construction industry. The same computing power that makes child's play of complex formulas makes it easy to overlook errors and entirely lose sight of the logic behind the numbers you entered into a formula. In addition, you will want much of the information in the *Planner* at your fingertips when you are on the jobsite and as you visit suppliers and subcontractors. Waiting for you to "boot-up, look-up and figure out" a calculation or estimate disrupts work and does not inspire confidence among the people who are bidding or working for you. My advice is to stick with paper for the field. Use the computer for playing with scheduling and estimating scenarios if you have time and understand the software.

This page is intentionally blank

I Specifications & Bid Preparation

I. Using Specifications and Bid Preparation

Procedure Summary

In this section you will determine specifications, identify potential subcontractors or suppliers and submit Requests for Quotation to gather price information that will be used in Section II to prepare a cost estimate and in section IV to arrange your construction schedule. The overall procedure in this section is:

1. Complete and duplicate Cover Page.
2. Complete and duplicate Requests for Quotation.
3. Identify potential subcontractors and suppliers and complete Subcontractor/ Supplier Records for each.
4. Send Cover Page and Request for Quotation to appropriate subcontractor or supplier noting the date sent and to whom in the Bid Log.
5. Enter date as completed bids are received.

Use the information in the next several pages to help in preparing and submitting Requests for Quotation.

About the Forms

This section contains three types of forms: **Requests for Quotation (RFQ), Subcontractor/Supplier Record** and **Bid Log**. There is an RFQ for each of the major areas where you are likely to use a subcontractor. In addition, there is a Cover Sheet containing basic information about your project that a subcontractor needs to know in order to bid accurately. The Subcontractor/Supplier Record is used for recording contact and business information about subcontractors or suppliers. The Bid Log helps you keep track of what RFQs have been sent, to whom and when and whether the recipient has responded.

The blueprints and materials list prepared by your log provider will not contain all of the detail necessary to accurately bid your project. It may not show where you intend to put carpeting or ceramic tile floors, or the color, type and grade of flooring materials. While your blueprints will show the locations of plumbing and lighting fixtures, they usually will not show the brand, model, style or color. Such details are part of the **Specifications** for your log home. These are important in obtaining an accurate bid from a subcontractor or supplier.

Start by completing the Request for Quotation Cover Page. This contains basic information about when and where you are building and how to contact you. Duplicate the completed form and attach a copy to all of the RFQs you send out. If you change building sites or contact information, send a revised Cover Sheet to everyone who has received an RFQ (recorded in your Bid Log).

Complete the Request for Quotations and then duplicate them, keeping a copy in your Project Planner and sending copies with cover sheet attached to appropriate subcontractors. By completing the form before making copies, you insure that subs and suppliers receive the same information. This insures that you are comparing "apples to apples" when you review competing bids.

Some RFQs ask for manufacturer, model, style and color. You can obtain this information by visiting building supply stores, checking catalogs or talking with friends and professionals. In some cases, you may prefer to let the subcontractor provide this information. In such cases, simply note on the RFQ: "Please specify" to insure that subs provide the information in their bids. For example, you may prefer to have your plumber select the brand and size of well pump and pressure tank for your home. This is perfectly acceptable, but you should ask what brand they intend to use so you can verify, if necessary, that it is from a reputable manufacturer.

Identifying Potential Subcontractors

Once you have completed the RFQs you will need to identify the potential subcontractors you want to bid on your project. Selection of subcontractors is as much art as science and there is an element of luck as well. The more thoroughly you research subcontractors, however, the more likely you are to have a smooth, efficient construction project that finishes on time and on budget. Always be sure you:

- Obtain and check references from previous clients
- Obtain a bank reference so you can check payment history
- Obtain and verify any licenses
- Obtain a Certificate of Insurance

There are several ways to build a list of potential subcontractors and suppliers. One method is to find an excellent reference for one of the subs, such as a trim carpenter or painter, whose work comes near completion of the house. Work backwards, asking those subs for recommendations for subcontractors who work ahead of them. For example, find a highly recommended finish carpenter and ask him to recommend good framing carpenters or ask a good painter about good drywall finishers. Once you've identified a reputable drywall finisher, ask him about a drywall hanger. Then ask the hanger about a framing carpenter. Ask the framing carpenter about a good foundation subcontractor and so on. You can refer to the Construction Schedule in Section IV and start with the subcontractors whose work appears near the bottom of the page, working your way up the page from there.

This method works well because the quality of many subcontractors' work as well as their work efficiency and profitability depends on the subcontractors who have come before them in the project. Poor carpentry in the interior framing of a log home creates a nightmare for the plumber, electrician, HVAC subcontractor, drywall hanger and trim carpenter. They are usually more than willing to recommend a sub whose workmanship has made their work smoother and of higher quality.

Even when a sub comes highly recommended, you should perform a basic background check and verify licenses and insurance. Construction is a highly volatile field and circumstances for subs can change drastically. Especially avoid any sub who lacks proper licensing, no matter what kind of bargain they are offering. Never use uninsured subs on your jobsite. Work injuries are not uncommon and as General Contractor, most states will hold you accountable for jobsite injuries of anyone you employ.

Submitting Requests for Quotation

As you identify potential subs, complete a Subcontractor/Supplier Record form for them. There is space on the form for special notes. Send each of your candidate subs the Cover Sheet and Request for Quotation for their particular trade. Include a copy of your blueprints or at least a preliminary floorplan and elevations. It's a good idea to advise subs that they will soon receive a Request for Quotation from you. Then follow up with a phone call to make sure your request arrived.

As you send out RFQs, record them in the Bid Log. As you receive bids, note them in the Log. If you modify a bid, treat it as a new bid and note in the "Received" column of the original Request, that the Request was replaced by a new one. Use the Bid Log to follow up on outstanding bids. Many subcontractors are much better about their trades than they are about following up on RFQs. However, if repeated calls to a subcontractor do not produce results, take that as a warning that their punctuality on the job may also be poor.

Tips on Getting Accurate Bids

Evaluate your bids carefully as you receive them. Make sure they contain all of the information you requested. If you have questions, contact the sub immediately. If one bid in a group is exceptionally high or low, contact the sub immediately and review it with them. Make sure they clearly understand your request. Until you have reviewed the bid, you can't be sure what is causing the price difference. Before signing a bid that contains a great price, make sure that the price is not the result of the subcontractor leaving out something that you wanted included. Never assume that a subcontractor is obligated to provide everything in your Request For Quotation, even if it isn't mentioned in their bid. It's the bid that counts, so be sure it contains everything you requested or references your Request For Quotation. For example, one plumber's bid may say "Plumbing for _____ residence as per Request For Quotation dated _____." Another's bid may list every item you had in your Request. Make sure your Request is accurate and complete before you send it and then make sure the bids are consistent with your Requests.

In some instances, a sub may insist on providing certain items that you have specified that you would provide. There are several reasons for this: The sub may purchase the items wholesale and rely on the marked up resale of that item to you for part of his income. This may not be as much of a problem as it might seem. Most subcontractors have relationships with suppliers. Often they can obtain items used in their trade at a better price than an individual homeowner. So even with a markup going to the sub, the cost will be no greater than if you had purchased and provided the materials and they provided only the labor to install them.

There are two other reasons often behind a sub's insistence that they provide materials in their subcontract. Providing materials gives them control over delivery and material quality. Every sub who has worked with an owner-contractor has experienced arriving on a jobsite to find that the owner-contractor does not have the necessary materials available. This represents a serious loss of time and money to the sub. In such situations, they will usually move to the next available job on their calendar (good subs are always busy) and move your project to the bottom of their work schedule. Most subs have also experienced a homeowner who found a "bargain" on some item that is really fit only for a landfill. The sub knows that installation likely will be difficult and that, as installer, they will also be assuming some warranty responsibility. Many subs have manufacturer or brand preferences and prefer to use these items or their equivalent in their work.

If subs insist on providing their own materials, ask them to specify the manufacturer, make, model, style and color of the items they will provide. Don't assume that subs are going to automatically include in their bids the level of quality that you want. Competition between subcontractors is intense and every sub knows when preparing a bid that every dollar added over the minimum necessary to do the work requested increases the chances that they will be underbid. Costs for a single toilet range from $100 to over $1,000 and they all perform the same function. Unless you specify your wishes, the sub is not obligated to provide anything beyond what's necessary to accomplish the intended task.

Don't send Requests For Quotation unless you have substantially completed blueprints, preliminary approval on financing and a reasonably definite construction start date. To be valid in the construction industry, bids usually must be accepted within 30 days and the work completed in 60-90 days. The exact terms are usually stated on the bid. A bid obtained six months or a year before starting construction is likely to be inaccurate and will probably not be enforceable anyway. For preliminary planning, you can request estimates from subcontractors and ask for their availability at the time you plan to start construction. Even if they honor a long-range bid, many subs have certain busy seasons and may be unavailable to start work when you need them.

Cover Page

Subcontract for: _____ Date of Request: _____

Name _____ Home Phone: _____
Mailing Address: _____
City: _____ State: _____ Zip: _____

Jobsite Address: _____
City: _____ State: _____ Zip: _____

Job Site Directions: _____

_____

_____

_____

_____

_____

_____

_____

_____

Please provide a firm bid to perform the work described in the attached specifications, including all materials, labor, taxes and permit fees for the items checked. Please include manufacturer, model numbers and color/styles (if not stated) where requested.

Excavation

Project: _____ Date: _____

Contact: _____ Phone: _____

_____ Clear/grade road
　　　_____ Spread gravel　　_____ Roll/compact

_____ Install drainage pipes/culverts

_____ Clear site
　　　_____ Remove stumps, debris

_____ Excavate for foundation (excavation within 1" of level)

_____ Backfill and rough grade

_____ Finish Grade

Special Instructions:

_____ Mark underground utilities

_____ Store topsoil separately

Remarks:

_____
_____
_____
_____
_____
_____
_____
_____
_____

Foundation

Project: _____	Date: _____
Contact: _____	Phone: _____

_____ Lay out footings/foundation

_____ Dig/form/pour footings

_____ Install foundation walls according to blueprints

Holes in foundation wall for SEPTIC, WATER, ELECTRICY TELEPHONE

_____ Poured Concrete _____ Block _____ Wood _____ Other

_____ Install foundation slab

_____ Install foundation drainage including drain tile, sump crock

_____ Apply waterproofing as specified below

_____ Install anchor bolts in top of foundation walls as specified in blueprints

_____ Install driveways and patios according to owner/builder specifications

Remarks:

Schedule any necessary inspections
Bid is for materials and labor
No more than 30 minutes between concrete pours to avoid cold joints
Concrete protected from freezing

Other _____

_____
_____
_____
_____

Logwork/Rough Carpentry

Project: _____   Date: _____

Contact: _____   Phone: _____

_____ Permit(s)

_____ Install subfloor system as per blueprints

_____ Install log wall system according to manufacturer's specifications

_____ Install exterior partition framing (plates, studs, blocking, sheathing)

_____ Install windows and exterior doors as per blueprints
      _____ Install windows and exterior door exterior trim as per blueprints
      _____ Install windows and exterior door interior trim as per blueprints

_____ Install second story floor system as per blueprints

_____ Install dormer framing (see headings for walls, roofs & gables)

_____ Install enclosure framing (fireplace/chimney, whirlpool tubs,
           built-in cabinets/pantries)

_____ Install interior partition framing as per blueprints

_____ Install ceiling framing (joists, braces)

_____ Install porches and decks (joists, ceiling joists, ledgers, bands, supports, deck
           ing, rafters, sheathing,)

_____ Roof System (as per blueprints)
      _____ Conventional framing
      _____ Built-up roof system
      _____ Combination
      _____ Install roof framing (rafters, flyrafters, blocking, ridgeboards, beams,
           felt paper, drip edge)

_____ Install shingles/ roof covering as specified on blueprints

_____ Install gable framing (plates, studs, blocking)

(over)

_____ Install log gables

_____ Install soffit framing as specified on blueprints

_____ Install soffit covering as specified on blueprints

_____ Install exterior log siding on walls and gables as specified on blueprints

_____ Install interior log siding on walls and gables as specified on blueprints

_____ Install interior t&g wall and ceiling coverings as specified on blueprints

_____ Install basement stairs as specified on blueprints
        _____Site-built _____Pre-fabricated unit

_____ Install finish stairs as specified on blueprints
        _____Site-built _____Pre-fabricated unit

Plumbing

Project: _____	Date: _____
Contact: _____	Phone: _____

_____ Permit(s)

_____ Public Water   Hook-up Allowance: _____

_____ Public Sewer   Hook-up Allowance: _____

_____ Heating System
        _____Hot Water Baseboard   _____Natural Gas
        _____Propane   _____Oil

_____ Well pump/ tank (specify make/model/size)
        _____Well   Depth: _____ Distance to House: _____

_____ Septic Hook-up   Distance to House: _____
        Water Lines _____PVC _____Copper
        Waste Lines _____PVC _____Iron

_____ Sump Pump

_____ Basement floor drain
        Basement Bath _____rough-in _____finished

_____ Sewage ejector pump

_____ Hot Water Heater(s)   Qty: _____Size: _____
                            Qty: _____Size: _____

_____ Kitchen Sink   Type: _____Size:_____

_____ Kitchen Sink Faucet   Type: _____   _____w/Spray

_____ Disposal (specify make/model/size)

_____ Instant Hot

_____ Ice Maker

(over)

_____ Bath fixtures

    _____ Toilets   Type: _____ Color: _____
    _____ Lav Sinks   Type: _____ Color: _____
    _____ Showers   Type: _____ Color: _____
    _____ Tubs   Type: _____ Color: _____
    _____ Shwr/Tub   Type: _____ Color: _____
    _____ Shwr/Tub Doors   Type: _____ Color: _____
    _____ Lav. Faucets   Type: _____ Color: _____
    _____ Shwr Diverters   Type: _____ Color: _____
    _____ Tub Faucets   Type: _____ Color: _____

_____ Master Bath

    _____ Toilet   Type: _____ Color: _____
    _____ Lav Sinks   Type: _____ Color: _____
    _____ Shower   Type: _____ Color: _____
    _____ Tub   Type: _____ Color: _____
    _____ Shwr/Tub   Type: _____ Color: _____
    _____ Shwr/Tub Drs.   Type: _____ Color: _____
    _____ Lav. Fauc.   Type: _____ Color: _____
    _____ Shower Diverter   Type: _____ Color: _____
    _____ Tub Faucets   Type: _____ Color: _____
    _____ Whirlpool/Jacuzzi Type: _____ Color: _____
    _____ Washing Machine Hook-up   Location: _____

Other _____

_____
_____
_____
_____
_____
_____
_____
_____
_____
_____

Heating and Cooling (HVAC)

Project: _____ Date: _____

Contact: _____ Phone: _____

_____ Install heating/ cooling system, including all inside/outside units,
necessary ductwork, thermostats, condensate drain lines

_____zones

_____ air-to-air heat pump
_____ groundsource heat pump
_____ electric forced air heat
_____ gas forced-air heat
_____ oil heat
_____ in-slab radiant heat
_____ air-conditioning
_____ humidifier
other (specify)_____

_____ Specify manufacturer, model and size for heating/cooling units.

_____ Install ventilation ductwork for:

_____ bath fans
_____ kitchen range hood
_____ downdraft range/grill ventilation
_____ dryer vent

_____ Include ventilation fans/ controls

*Remarks:*_____

_____

_____

_____

_____

_____

_____

_____

_____

Electrical

Project: _____ Date: _____

Contact: _____ Phone: _____

—————— Service Panel:
_200_ Amp.   —————— Temporary Pole/Service Panel

—————— Heating System
    ——————Electric Baseboard   —————— Heat Pump(s)   —————— amp
    ——————Forced Air electric   —————— Gas/ Oil
    ——————Outside A/C disconnect   —————— amp

—————— Permit(s)

—————— Total receptacles (includes those listed below)

—————— Switched outlets

—————— Brass floor outlets

—————— Weatherproof outlets

—————— Smoke detectors

—————— Phone outlets   ——————Number of lines

—————— Cable TV outlets   —————— attic termination for antenna

—————— Computer Network Wiring (diagram provided)

—————— Floodlights   ——————Motion Sensor(s)

—————— Paddle Fan/Lights   —————— Assemble and hang

—————— Lights in Beams

—————— Outlets in log walls

—————— Bath Light/Fan Units

—————— Recessed Lights

(over)

—————— Pull Chain / Keyless Light Fixtures

—————— Heat Lamps

—————— Closet lights with wall switch   ————————Use flourescent fixtures

—————— Intercom

—————— Well pump/ tank   ————————Sump Pump ————Sewage ejector pump

—————— Hot Water Heater(s)   Qty: _____ Size: _____

—————— Disposal   ————————Instant Hot Water ————Ice Maker

—————— Range/oven   ————————Microwave Oven ————Cook-Top

—————— Whirlpool/Sauna

—————— Washing Machine   ————————Dryer

—————— Door Chimes: ————————Front Door ————Back door

—————— Price to hang light fixtures $_____per fixture

—————— Wire chases, holes and receptacles in logs and beams will be drilled or routed by carpenters, wire will be laid in beam chases by builder according to electricians specifications; wire to be provided by electrician.

—————— Other _____

—————— Other _____

*Remarks:*_____

_____

_____

_____

_____

_____

Drywall

Project: _____	Date: _____
Contact: _____	Phone: _____

_____ Include all materials and delivery in bid

_____ Hang drywall as per blueprints

_____ Finish drywall as per specifications below

_____ Walls should be fastened with glue and: _____ nails _____ screws

_____ Ceilings should be glued and secured with screws

_____ All fasteners set below surface

_____ Joints should be taped and finished with three coats of joint compound with each coat sanded.

_____ All outside corners reinforced with metal corner bead

_____ All inside corners reinforced with joint tape

_____ All cutouts in drywall including doors, windows, electrical outlets and fixtures, HVAC ducts

_____ Use water-resistant gypsum board (around showers, tubs and any areas susceptible to moisture

*Remarks:*_____

_____

_____

_____

_____

_____

Paint/Stain/Varnish/Seal

Project: _____	Date: _____
Contact: _____	Phone: _____

_____ **Furnish materials**

_____ **Apply exterior sealant to logs**

_____ **Apply exterior sealant/paint to exterior trim**

_____ **Caulk/Chink exterior log joints as specified below**

_____ **Caulk/Chink interior log joints as specified below**

_____ **Stain/finish interior logs and beams as specified below**

_____ **Stain/finish interior tongue and groove as specified below**

_____ **Stain/finish interior trim**

_____ **Paint drywall according to attached finish schedule**

_____ **Apply wallpaper as specified in attached finish schedule**

Remarks:

- *Unless noted above, materials will be furnished*
- *Sealant applied according to manufacturer's recommendations*
- *Paint, sealant, caulking, chinking applied according to manufacturer's recommendations*
- *All drywall surface primed and _____ coats of finish*
- *Walls touch sanded after primer*
- *Colors and paint type as shown on the finish schedule*
- *Trim joints caulked and sanded before painting*
- *Window panes cleaned by painter*
- *Excess paint remains on site*
- *Other _____*

_____

_____

_____

Trim Carpentry

Project: _____ Date: _____

Contact: _____ Phone: _____

_____ Set/trim interior doors
      _____ pre-hung interior doors   _____ hung on site/site-built jambs

_____ Set/trim windows as specified by owner/builder

_____ Install base, crown, chair rail

_____ Install tongue and groove, raised panels, wainscoting as shown on blueprints

_____ Install closet shelves and rods

_____ Install/trim stairs and rails
      _____ stair/railing stock provided   _____ pre-manufactured stairs/rails

_____ Install special trim as specified by owner/builder

_____ Install doorknobs/locksets, deadbolts, doorstops, and window hardware

_____ All trim installed using finish nails, set below surface, puttied and sanded smooth

_____ Trim carpenter to provide nails

BID LOG

Subcontract	Subcontractor	Contact	Address	Phone	Bid Sent	Bid Recvd.

II Cost Estimating

II. Detailed Cost Estimating

Procedure Summary

In this section, you will prepare an accurate estimate of the cost of your log home using individual **Cost Detail Sheets**. When you transfer totals for each Detail Sheet to the **Cost Summary Sheet**, you will be able to calculate the total cost for your project. Start by duplicating the detail sheets. This will preserve your originals in case you need to re-do a sheet or want to do comparisons.

1. Duplicate Cost Detail and Summary Sheets, work with copies.
2. Use Detail Sheets to fill in estimated costs (pencil works best).
3. Replace estimated figures with bids as you accept them.
4. Use supporting worksheets and schedules where noted on individual Detail Sheets to calculate material requirements.
5. Enter totals from Cost Detail Sheet on Cost Summary Sheet and calculate total cost of your project.

Using the Cost Detail Sheets

Each Cost Detail Sheet covers a specific part of the construction of your log home. Detail Sheets contain five parts. Part I is the actual Cost Detail and is used to enter estimates or bid figures. Part II provides a place to record the Supplier or Subcontractor providing the figures used in Part I. Part III includes remarks and tips about the specific item covered by the detail sheet. Part IV contains formulas and examples that can be used when calculations are required. Part V is a blank area for recording notes and calculations. This allows you to return to a calculation quickly to review, modify or correct it. Note that on some Detail Sheets Parts III and IV may be empty. This is intentional and may be because they are not applicable for the specific detail or they involve calculations that should be performed by the subcontractor. Calculations and examples are included only when they involve labor and materials likely to be handled by a homeowner.

If you want to obtain a preliminary estimate, pencil item estimates into the Cost Detail Sheets and note the total in the box in the upper right hand corner. Recording with a pencil allows you to replace figures with more accurate bids or estimates as they become available. As an alternative, you can make two copies of the sheets, using one for a preliminary and one for a final estimate.

Not all projects require all of the Cost Details in the workbook. If a Cost Detail isn't required, write N/A (not applicable) in the total area for that Detail. (Confirm that the Detail isn't required before entering this. You may want to discuss it with a builder, subcontractor or building code official before excluding it.) In other cases, work broken into several cost centers may actually be covered in a single bid from one subcontractor. Record the bid in one of the Detail Sheets and write the Detail Number in the Total area for the other Detail Sheets that are included. For example, the three Cost Details: 320 Excavation, 370 Backfill and Rough Grading and 800 Final Grading are often covered in a single estimate or bid from an excavating subcontractor. Enter the inclusive bid on Detail Sheet 320. In the total area of the other two sheets, write "See 320". When all of the Detail Sheet totals contain either a total, "N/A" or a reference to another Detail Sheet, you are ready to build your Cost Summary.

Completing the Cost Summary

Enter individual totals into the appropriate place in the Cost Summary Sheet. If the Detail Sheet total contains an "N/A" or reference to another Detail Sheet, transfer that information to the appropriate total area on the Cost Summary Sheet. You are finished when all of the total areas of the Summary Sheet contain something. There should be no "holes" in the Summary Sheet. ("Holes" in a Cost Summary Sheet are places where large amounts of your money can disappear during construction. Close them before construction begins!)

Contingencies

Even with careful bidding and accurate estimating, many things can happen during a construction project that affect costs. It's important to include a "contingency" to cover unexpected costs. For example, based on a neighbor's or well-driller's experience, you may enter an estimate of $2,500 for a 200-foot well. Murphy's Law strikes and the driller finally hits water at 600 feet. The price tag of your well jumps to $6,000 or $3,500 over budget. (See "Estimates vs. Bids" for more information). A contingency helps cover such unexpected occurrences. Cost Detail 900 allows you to enter a project contingency. Subtotal your Cost Summary Sheet and use the instructions on Detail Sheet 920 to calculate a contingency. Then enter this into the appropriate area of the Cost Summary sheet. This appears on your Cost Summary Sheet immediately beneath the subtotal.

Regard your contingency as sacred. The tighter your budget, the more important it becomes. If you are operating at the upper limit of your financial ability, you need a larger contingency rather than a smaller one because the effects of substantial cost overruns can have more impact. Your contingency is like insurance against unknown costs. The more effort you put into preparing bid requests, selecting subcontractors and managing your project, the less likely you will be to use much of your contingency.

Don't start spending contingency funds until your project is complete and all the bills are paid. Throughout your project, you will have some items come in under budget and other items run over. Owner-contractors sometimes hurt themselves by dipping into the contingency when they see a few areas where they are under budget. Later they are hit by unexpected costs and have to struggle to cover them.

Estimates vs. Bids

A bid or price quotation is a document provided by a subcontractor or supplier that specifies a specific cost and provides detailed explanation of what is included in that cost. It is signed by the supplier or sub and is valid for them only. Obtaining a signed bid from one sub and assuming that price is good for all subs is a serious mistake. Follow this simple rule: "The only price that matters is the one signed by the person who will actually do the work. Everything else is an estimate."

In some cases, even a bid is really an estimate. Reading the fine print, you'll discover that there are a number of circumstances that override the bid and can result in extra charges. This particularly applies to activities related to site preparation and excavation. Even firm bids usually contain clauses allowing subs to charge extra if conditions aren't as they expect. Well drillers and excavators, for example, can rarely guarantee a price because they cannot predict what they will encounter beneath the ground surface. If an excavator strikes rock while digging your foundation, they will usually point out the "rock clause" in their contract that voids any fixed fees and specifies alternative pricing, usually an hourly or daily rate. This is another reason to include and respect a contingency.

Allowances

In some cases, a subcontractor may provide a bid without knowing what specific materials will be needed. Since they can't accurately calculate the costs of unknown materials, they make an educated guess called an allowance. For example, many people do not select lighting fixtures, floor coverings and cabinetry until construction is well under way. Yet the costs for these items must be accounted for in the cost estimate before construction starts (unless you won't be borrowing money for your project and don't mind the uncertainty).

In these situations, the subcontractor provides an allowance to cover the anticipated cost of the unknown items. An allowance for electricians and plumbers may include fixtures, realizing that you won't be selecting them for a while. Then when you select your fixtures, the sub purchases the materials. If your selection exceeds your allowance, they will invoice you for the difference.

Confirm that allowances are realistic in all bids. For example, an allowance of $1,000 for lighting fixtures in an elegant 4,000 square foot log home is plainly unrealistic unless you intend to just hang bare bulbs from the ceiling. Consider the items included in the allowance, estimate the quantity and costs for the type and quality you want and compare your figure with the allowance. If there is a large difference, either have the sub adjust the allowance or add the extra amount you anticipate to the bid to be sure you're covered.

Evaluating Bids

Try to obtain at least three bids for each Cost Detail that you are bidding. Review each bid carefully and compare it with the Request For Quotation you submitted. If any part of the bid is unclear, contact the sub before making a decision. There are a lot of jokes made about accepting the "low bid." These are made with reason. If a bid looks too good to be true it almost certainly is. If there is a wide range between the low and the high bid, it raises the possibility that you weren't clear about what you wanted in your Request for Quotation or some of the subs didn't understand. When bids range widely, review all of them with the subcontractors.

Make sure bids specifically state the items specified in your RFQ or reference to your blueprints and Request for Quotation. Sometimes instead of re-writing, the subcontractor will simply write on their bid form, "as per Request for Quotation dated ..." or "as per blueprints dated..." Bids that lack detail are land mines that will blow up your budget during construction.

Before selecting a bid, make sure the sub is properly licensed and insured. Ask for a Certificate of Insurance before work starts. Reputable subs expect this. You may want to call your local Better Business Bureau or the bank that handles the sub's business account. Be wary of subs who won't provide bank or personal references.

When you notify subs that you've accepted their bid, let them know when you anticipate starting construction. Find out how much lead time they require and the best time to call. Record these on the Subcontractor/Supplier Record Form. For suppliers, ask how much advance notice is required for deliveries. You will use this information in Section IV to develop your construction calendar. Be aware that some subs require an initial payment to begin work. The amount required and due date should be stated on their bid. The amount should not exceed 25%. Beware of subs who require half up front and half on delivery because they will be receiving some or all of their profit before they ever set foot on your jobsite. Don't make initial payments until the sub's portion of construction is imminent, usually 30 days or less in advance of their arrival on the jobsite. If possible, tell them you'll meet them with the initial payment check when they arrive on your jobsite.

Working With A Lender

If you will be working with a lending company, the lender will require a detailed cost estimate supported by signed subcontracts to verify the cost of construction. Your estimate will be compared with the appraised value of your project to determine the amount of money the lender will make available. Lenders often have their own cost breakdown forms, although many will accept the Cost Estimate Summary in the *Project Planner*. Show it to your lender when you apply for your loan.

Lenders usually disburse money for construction loans in a series of "draws" based on a percentage of completion of the project. In order for them to release money, they will need to verify that the work specified in the "draw schedule" has been completed. In some cases, a lender will release money in the construction loan account based on invoices received from subs. Draws based on percentage of completion are very general. Don't celebrate just because there's money left over after you've paid for all of the activities covered within a draw. A later draw will probably be less than required and you will need to have those funds available. Celebrate any savings only when construction is 100% complete and all invoices have been paid.

Log home owners often add custom features to their homes that add considerable cost. This may result in the cost exceeding the appraised value of your home. For example, a ground-source heat pump provides very energy efficient heating and cooling but costs three to five times more than an air-to-air heat pump. Unfortunately, the appraised value of the project won't be increased by the full cost difference if a ground-source heat pump is used. Adding too many such "big ticket" items can create problems getting a loan approval. If your budget gets tight, look first at those items you can pay for out of pocket. Then include only the basic cost in your Cost Estimate Summary and add the upgrades at your own expense. If budget becomes an issue, look at features you want that might be added later. Include basic lighting fixtures, carpeting instead of hardwood, and drywall instead of wood paneling. These items can be upgraded later when you have the cash and time and their cost won't damage your loan to value ratio.

Above all, don't try to fool the lender by padding costs to pay yourself or putting unrealistic figures into your Cost Estimate Summary. The lender will check your figures, but should they miss something, you are still liable for actual costs.

When you have completed your Cost Estimate Summary and secured financing, you are almost ready to begin construction. Go to Section IV to build your Construction Calendar.

210 Plans & Blueprints

Total: $_____

I. COST DETAIL

2101	Design Fees		_____
2102	Engineering/Architects Fees		_____
2103	Additional Blueprint Sets		_____
210	Total		_____

II. SUPPLIERS & SUBCONTRACTORS

Designer: _____

Contact: _____ Phone: _____

Engineering/Architect: _____

Contact: _____ Phone: _____

III. NOTES

Check with local building code officials to see if blueprints will require stamps or seals from licensed architect or engineer. If so, contact your log home provider to obtain estimate of fees or obtain estimate locally.

SEE STEVE

IV. FORMULAS & EXAMPLES

[Obtain a project cost from architects or engineers when using services not provided by your log producer. Use square foot costs for comparison only. Attempting to calculate costs from cost per square foot figures provided by suppliers may result in errors.]

V. CALCULATIONS

220 Permits/Fees

Total: $_____

I. COST DETAIL

2201	Building Permit		_____
2202	Zoning/Impact Fees		_____
2203	Stormwater Management		_____
2204	Septic		_____
2205	Well		_____
2206	Other_____		_____
2207	Other_____		_____
2208	Other_____		_____
220	Total		_____

II. SUPPLIERS & SUBCONTRACTORS

Building Code Authority_____

Contact: _____ **Phone:** _____

III. NOTES

Obtain fee schedule from local building code officials. Be aware that several agencies may be involved with each having their own fees. Ask if all fees are included in the information you are given.

Have subcontractors include fees for mechanical permits (electric, plumbing) in their bids.

IV. FORMULAS & EXAMPLES

V. CALCULATIONS

230 Sewer/Septic

	Total: $_____

I. COST DETAIL

A. **For home on municipal or community sewer system**

2301   Sewer Tap Fee   _____

2302   Sewer Line   _____

230a   Total Sewer   **_____**

B. **For home on septic system**

2303   Perc Test   _____

2304   Septic system subcontract   _____

230b   Total Septic   **_____**

II. SUPPLIERS & SUBCONTRACTORS

Septic Subcontractor: _____

Contact: _____ Phone: _____

Septic Permit Authority: _____

Contact: _____ Phone: _____

III. NOTES

Subcontract to install septic system includes all materials and labor for drainage field, tank, distribution boxes, pump or injector, if required and drain line from house to tank.

Complete only section A or B depending on your circumstance. Tap fees may be obtained from local or municipal authorities.

IV. FORMULAS & EXAMPLES

V. CALCULATIONS

240 Water/Well

Total: $ _____

I. COST DETAIL

A. **For houses connecting to municipal or community water:**

2401   Water Tap Fee   _____

2402   Water Line   _____

240a   Total   _____

B. **For houses requiring a private well:**

2403   Well Permit   _____
Permit is for drilling well, final water test may be required

2404   Well   _____
Subcontract for installation of well includes drilling, casing, grouting and testing

2405   Well Pump, tank   _____
Materials and labor to install well pump and pressure tank

2406   Well Line   _____
Materials and labor for installation of line from well to house

240b   Total   _____

II. SUPPLIERS & SUBCONTRACTORS

Well Driller: _____
Contact: _____ Phone: _____

Well Permit Authority: _____
Contact: _____ Phone: _____

III. NOTES

Complete only section A or B depending on your circumstance. Tap fees may be obtained from local or municipal authorities.

IV. FORMULAS & EXAMPLES

V. CALCULATIONS

250 Electric Service

Total: $ _____

I. COST DETAIL

2501 Electric service _____
Cost to bring electric service to house from nearest existing point, usually includes phone wire. Obtain an estimate from the utility company.

2502 Trenches,Poles, Conduit _____
Cost of trenches or poles not included in 2501. Also include materials such as PVC pipe, joints and pipe cement.

250 Total electric _____

II. SUPPLIERS & SUBCONTRACTORS

Utility Company: _____
Contact: _____ Phone: _____

III. NOTES

Obtain an estimate from your local utility company as early as possible in your project. Try to have service to the site by the time carpentry starts.

IV. FORMULAS & EXAMPLES

V. CALCULATIONS

260 Natural Gas/Propane*

Total: $ _____

I. COST DETAIL

A. Install Natural Gas from municipal line

2601   Natural Gas   _____
Install natural gas line from common pipe to house, does not include hook-up at house

2602   Connect gas line   _____
Connect natural gas line at house

260a   Total   _____

B. Install Propane Tank

2603   Set Propane tank   _____
Materials and labor to set propane tank including preparation of pad or base and delivery

2604   Connect Propane Tank   _____
Materials and labor to install line connecting propane tank to house

260b   Total   _____

II. SUPPLIERS & SUBCONTRACTORS

Natural Gas Supplier: _____

Contact: _____Phone: _____

Propane Supplier: _____

Contact: _____Phone: _____

III. NOTES

Complete either A or B depending on whether you will be connecting to natural gas service or installing a propane tank.

IV. FORMULAS & EXAMPLES

V. CALCULATIONS

270 Portable Toilet

Total: $ _____

I. COST DETAIL

2701 Portable Toilet rental
Rental of portable toilet for duration of construction or until inside plumbing is functional; usually includes regular cleaning

_____

2702 Delivery and pick-up

_____

270 **Total**

_____

II. SUPPLIERS & SUBCONTRACTORS

Portable Toilet Supplier: _____

Contact: _____ Phone: _____

III. NOTES

Obtain prices from portable toilet service. Look in Yellow Pages under "Toilet-Portable." Plan to have toilet on site throughout construction to avoid damage to house fixtures.

IV. FORMULAS & EXAMPLES

V. CALCULATIONS

Estimated time required (months)_____ X Rental fee _____per month = _____

280 Storage Van

Total: $_____

I. COST DETAIL

2801	Rental Fee		_____
2802	Deliver/Pick-up		_____
280	Total		_____

II. SUPPLIERS & SUBCONTRACTORS

Supplier: _____

Contact: _____ Phone: _____

III. NOTES

Use a storage trailer to protect delicate materials such as interior trim, doors, windows, hardware, cabinetry and appliances if dry storage isn't available at your jobsite. Look in the Yellow Pages under "Storage" for sources.

IV. FORMULAS & EXAMPLES

V. CALCULATIONS

Estimated time required (months)_____X Rental fee _____ per month = _____

300 Clearing/Site Preparation* | Total: $ _____ |

I. COST DETAIL

3001	Mowing	_____
3002	Mark, drop trees	_____
3003	Cut, stack firewood	_____
3004	Chip/remove tops	_____

Materials and labor to chip tops

| 3005 | Remove stumps | _____ |

Load, haul stumps

| 3006 | Demolition | _____ |

Dismantle, remove structures

| 3007 | Remove trash/debris | _____ |

Hauling, landfill fees

| 300 | Total | _____ |

II. SUPPLIERS & SUBCONTRACTORS

Subcontractor: _____

Contact: _____ Phone: _____

III. NOTES

Sometimes the excavator simply clears the building area as the first step in excavation. In this case, the cost of clearing may be incorporated in the excavation costs.

Be sure to include rental costs for any equipment you may use yourself in preparing your site.

IV. FORMULAS & EXAMPLES

V. CALCULATIONS

310 Lot Layout

Total: $_____

I. COST DETAIL

3101	Stake house location	_____
	Stake house, install batter boards	
3102	Stake road	_____
3103	Mark well	_____
3104	Stake septic location	_____
310	Total	_____

II. SUPPLIERS & SUBCONTRACTORS

Subcontractor: _____

Contact: _____ Phone: _____

III. NOTES

House layout may be done by surveyor, foundation contractor or builder. If you plan to have one of these subcontractors do the layout, be sure to include it in their subcontract. Do not complete this page if layout costs are covered in other subcontracts.

IV. FORMULAS & EXAMPLES

V. CALCULATIONS

320 Excavating*

| Total: $ _____ |

I. COST DETAIL

3201   **Excavate foundation**   _____
Estimated cost of excavating. May be entered as a subcontract or estimate. (See note)

3202   **Equipment pickup/delivery**   _____
Cost to pick up and deliver machinery.

320   **Total**   _____

II. SUPPLIERS & SUBCONTRACTORS

Subcontractor: _____
Contact: _____ Phone: _____

III. NOTES

Excavators often work by the hour instead of subcontracting. Ask for hourly rates and an estimate of how much time to anticipate. Ask for haul charges to remove stumps or debris and charges to pick up and deliver equipment.

IV. FORMULAS & EXAMPLES

V. CALCULATIONS

Loader hourly rate _____ X _____ *hours estimated =* _____

330 Footings

Total: $_____

I. COST DETAIL

3301   **Excavate footings**
Subcontract or estimate to mark, excavate footings   _____

3302   **Piers/fireplace footings**   _____

3303   **Equipment pickup/delivery**   _____
Deliver and pick up equipment

330   **Total**   **_____**

II. SUPPLIERS & SUBCONTRACTORS

Footings Supplier: _____
Contact: _____ **Phone:** _____

Subcontractor: _____
Contract: _____ **Phone:** _____

III. NOTES

Footings may be either dug using a backhoe or formed with lumber. Price for footings is sometimes given as a cost per linear foot, depending on the footing width and depth. If you will use a full service foundation contractor, they may include cost of the footings in the foundation cost. Linear foot costs should include reinforcing steel and other items specified on the blueprints.

Piers and special footings are usually calculated separately. Ask the footing or foundation sub. Be sure reinforcing steel and other blueprint specs are followed.

IV. FORMULAS & EXAMPLES

V. CALCULATIONS

340 Foundation

Total: $ _____

I. COST DETAIL

3401   Install Foundation   _____
Subcontract for materials and labor to install foundation,
including foundation walls, drain tile, waterproofing

3402   Other   _____
(specify)

3403   Other   _____
(specify)

340   Total   _____

II. SUPPLIERS & SUBCONTRACTORS

Subcontractor: _____

Contact: _____ Phone: _____

Foundation Suppliers: _____

Contact: _____ Phone: _____

III. NOTES

Foundation total should be for complete foundation as shown on foundation
plan. If you will be providing any part of the foundation, such as drain tile or
waterproofing, enter estimated amounts on lines labeled "Other" and show
calculations on next page.

IV. FORMULAS & EXAMPLES

V. CALCULATIONS

350 Steel

Total: $ _____

I. COST DETAIL

350   **Structural steel**   _____
Steel girder for subfloor system, special steel, includes delivery

II. SUPPLIERS & SUBCONTRACTORS

Steel Supplier: _____

Contact: _____ **Phone:** _____

III. NOTES

If using steel girder(s), obtain cost from supplier, including delivery.

Include steel support posts with subfloor system.

IV. FORMULAS & EXAMPLES

V. CALCULATIONS

360 Termite Treatment

Total: $_____

I. COST DETAIL

360 **Pre-treat for termites** _____
Soil/foundation pre-treatment by licensed applicator

II. SUPPLIERS & SUBCONTRACTORS

Treatment Subcontractor: _____

Contact: _____ Phone: _____

III. NOTES

In termite areas, lenders usually require proof of termite pre-treatment before releasing construction loan proceeds.

IV. FORMULAS & EXAMPLES

V. CALCULATIONS

370 Backfill/Rough Grading

Total: $ _____

I. COST DETAIL

3701   Backfill/rough grade foundation
Backfill/rough grade foundation according to specifications   _____

3702   Equipment pickup/delivery
Deliver/pick up equipment   _____

370   **Total**   _____

II. SUPPLIERS & SUBCONTRACTORS

Subcontractor: _____

Contact: _____   Phone: _____

III. NOTES

Excavation work is usually priced by the hour for equipment and operator. Ask for an hourly rate and estimate for time required to do work. If subcontracting excavation, have excavator include backfill, rough grading and finish grading in their subcontract.

Excavators usually charge for equipment delivery and pick-up. Be sure to include these charges when estimating. If subcontracting, have excavator include equipment moving charges.

IV. FORMULAS & EXAMPLES

V. CALCULATIONS

_____ *hours @* _____*per hour =* _____

380 Gravel Fill

Total: $ _____

I. COST DETAIL

380   **Gravel Fill**
Gravel for drain tile surrounding foundation, base for foundation slab, if not included in concrete flatwork

_____

II. SUPPLIERS & SUBCONTRACTORS

Gravel Supplier: _____

Contact: _____ Phone: _____

III. NOTES

Gravel is used for road beds, foundations, and beneath walks and slabs. Whenever possible have subcontractors include gravel in their bids. Estimate gravel quantities below.

Estimate gravel quantities at 1.5 ton per cubic yard

Obtain gravel prices from local quarry, prices vary with stone type

Gravel is usually delivered in 10 or 20 ton dump trucks. Divide tons by truck size to estimate number of trucks.

IV. FORMULAS & EXAMPLES

(length in feet x width in feet x depth in feet /27) X 1.5 = tons gravel

Example:

How much gravel is required to make a 6" base for a 10' drive, 200' long?

.5 ft x 10 ft x 200 ft = 1000/27 =37.3 cubic yards gravel

How many 20 ton truck loads?

37.3 cubic yards/20 = 1.85 =2 20 ton truck load(s)

V. CALCULATIONS

400 Log Package, incl. delivery

Total: $ _____

I. COST DETAIL

4001   **Log Package**   _____
All components included in sales agreement

4002   **Delivery**   _____
Delivery to job site if not included in package agreement

400   **Total**   _____

II. SUPPLIERS & SUBCONTRACTORS

Log Home Company:_____

Contact: _____Phone: _____

III. NOTES

Package price includes any change orders, additions or deletions.

Delivery includes cost to transport package from manufacturer to job site only. Do not include unloading charges or forklift rental.

IV. FORMULAS & EXAMPLES

V. CALCULATIONS

410 Unloading Logs

Total: $ _____

I. COST DETAIL

4101   **Forklift rental**   _____
Rental including delivery and pickup

4102   **Other equipment rental**   _____
Other equipment required, including delivery

4103   **Unloading labor**   _____
Hired labor for unloading

410   **Total**   _____

II. SUPPLIERS & SUBCONTRACTORS

Forklift Supplier: _____
Contact: _____ **Phone:** _____

III. NOTES

If entrance road is inaccessible by trucks delivering package, a smaller truck may be required to transport materials to job site.

Packages using large logs or beams may require a crane instead of or in addition to a forklift.

If possible, have carpenter or logsmith include unloading labor in their subcontract.

IV. FORMULAS & EXAMPLES

Daily forklift rental rate _____ X _____ *days rental =* _____

Forklift delivery and pickup _____ X _____ *trips =* _____

V. CALCULATIONS

415 Crane, equipment rental

Total: $ _____

I. COST DETAIL

4106	Crane rental	_____
4107	Backhoe rental	_____
4108	Bobcat rental	_____
4109	Front end loader	_____
4200	Other *(specify)*	_____
415	Total	_____

II. SUPPLIERS & SUBCONTRACTORS

Equipment Supplier: _____

Contact: _____ Phone: _____

III. NOTES

Use this page to calculate rental equipment needs for the job. Discuss these with carpenter or builder. Use construction schedule to determine when machines are needed and for how long.

Try to minimize the number of trips required to reduce pick up/delivery charges.

IV. FORMULAS & EXAMPLES

Use the general formula:

time rented X rental rate + pickup/delivery charges = total rental

V. CALCULATIONS

420 Windows/Doors not in pkg

Total: $____

I. COST DETAIL

4201 **Windows not in package**   _____
Enter total from Window Worksheet

4202 **Doors not in package**   _____
Enter total from Door Worksheet

420 **Total**   _____

II. SUPPLIERS & SUBCONTRACTORS

Window Supplier: _____
Contact: _____ Phone: _____

Door Supplier: _____
Contact: _____ Phone: _____

III. NOTES

Use the Window/Door Worksheet to itemize doors and windows that aren't included in the log package. Enter totals above.

IV. FORMULAS & EXAMPLES

V. CALCULATIONS

430 Framing Materials not in pkg

Total: $_____

I. COST DETAIL

430   **Framing materials not in package**
      Enter total fromFraming Materials Worksheet   _____

II. SUPPLIERS & SUBCONTRACTORS

Building Materials Supplier: _____
Contact: _____ **Phone:** _____

III. NOTES

Use the Framing Materials Worksheet to itemize materials that aren't included in the log package.

Be sure to include nails, screws, adhesives and other fasteners.

IV. FORMULAS & EXAMPLES

V. CALCULATIONS

440 Logwork/Framing Labor

Total: $_____

I. COST DETAIL

440   Logwork/Framing Labor Total
Subcontract for logs, beams, interior framing, set doors, windows

_____

II. SUPPLIERS & SUBCONTRACTORS

Subcontractor: _____

Contract: _____ Phone: _____

III. NOTES

Obtain a bid from carpenter, builder or log builder using the Carpentry Request for Quotation.

Be sure subcontract does not include work that you intend to perform.

For preliminary cost estimating ask subcontractors for an approximate cost per square foot. Use this figure cautiously! Make sure your final decision is based on a firm bid rather than an estimate.

IV. FORMULAS & EXAMPLES

V. CALCULATIONS

500 Masonry/Stone

Total: $_____

I. COST DETAIL

A. Subcontract

500a   Masonry Subcontract
*Subcontract for masonry for walks, walls, fireplaces,
foundation coverings, but not foundation itself*   _____

B. Labor and Materials Pricing

5001   Masonry Materials
*Stone, artificial stone, block, mortar, sand, reinforcing
steel, mesh*   _____

5002   Masonry Labor

500b   Total   _____

II. SUPPLIERS & SUBCONTRACTORS

Subcontractor: _____

Contact: _____ Phone: _____

Masonry Materials Supplier: _____

Contact: _____ Phone: _____

III. NOTES

*Obtain a bid from a mason based on blueprints. Use pictures from scrapbook to
illustrate.*

Be sure subcontract does not include work that you intend to perform.

*For preliminary cost estimating, ask subcontractors for an approximate cost per
square foot. Use this figure cautiously! Make sure the final estimate includes a
firm bid rather than an estimate.*

IV. FORMULAS & EXAMPLES

Square feet of natural stonework _____ X _____ *cost/SF* = _____

Square feet of artificial stonework _____ X _____ *cost/SF* = _____

Square feet of masonry blockwork _____ X _____ *cost/SF* = _____

V. CALCULATIONS

510 Roofing Material not in pkg

Total: $ _____

I. COST DETAIL

5101   **Coverings**   _____
Shingles, metal, tile, drip edge, fasteners

5102   **Sheathing**   _____
Plywood, t&g decking, nails

5103   **Framing**   _____
Dimensional lumber, timbers, nails

5104   **Flashing**   _____

510   **Total**   _____

II. SUPPLIERS & SUBCONTRACTORS

Roofing Material Supplier: _____
Contact: _____ **Phone:** _____

III. NOTES

Use the Roof Materials Worksheet to calculate the cost of materials not included in your log home package.

If you are unfamiliar with roof construction, take your blueprints to a lumber yard or roofing company and they can perform take-offs and provide a materials estimate.

Estimate flashing directly from blueprints. Calculate for chimneys, dormers, skylights, etc.

IV. FORMULAS & EXAMPLES

Squares of Shingles = SF Roof Area/100 +10% waste
Bundles of Starter Shingle = (LF Eaves+ 10% waste)/80
Bundles of Ridge = LF Ridges/33
Rolls of Roofing Felt = SF Roof Area/400 + 10% waste
Drip Edge = LF Roof Edge + 10%
Lbs. 1-1/4" Roofing Nails = 2 x Squares of Shingles
Sheets of 4'x8' Sheathing = (SF Roof area + 5% waste)/32

V. CALCULATIONS

(Use Roof Factor Table to calculate roof area from flat roof plan)

<u>Shingles:</u> *SF Roof Area* _____ */ 100 + 10% =* _____ *squares of shingles*

Starters: $\dfrac{\text{LF eaves } + 10\%}{80}$ = _____ *Bndle fiberglass shingles*

Ridge: $\dfrac{\text{LF Ridges}}{33}$ = _____ *Bndle fiberglas shingles*

Felt: *SF Roof Area* _____ */ 400 + 10% =* _____ *rolls 15# felt*

(Double number of rolls if using 30# felt)

Drip Edge: *LF Roof Edge* _____ *+ 10% =* _____ *LF Drip Edge*

Nails: *2 X* _____ *squares shingles =* _____ *lbs. 1-1/4″ galv roof nails*

Sheathing: (SF Roof area _____ *+ 5%)/32 =* _____ *sheets of sheathing*

520 Roofing Labor

Total: $ _____

I. COST DETAIL

5201 **Roof Covering Labor** _____
Subcontract for installing roof coverings

5202 **Roof Framing Labor** _____
Subcontract for roof framing, installing soffits, fascia and eaves

520 **Total** _____

II. SUPPLIERS & SUBCONTRACTORS

Covering Subcontractor: _____
Contact: _____ Phone: _____

Framing Subcontractor: _____
Contact: _____ Phone: _____

III. NOTES

Obtain bid from roofing subcontractor. Carpenters and builders often install roof coverings also. If carpenter installs roofing, cost may be included on carpentry bid.

Be sure subcontract does not include work that you intend to perform.

Roofing subcontractors often estimate using cost per square of shingles. This can provide a rough estimate. Ask what is included. Use this figure cautiously! Make sure your final decision is based on a firm bid rather than an estimate.

Soffit and fascia are often installed by carpenters as part of the carpentry sub-contract. However these may also be done by a separate subcontractor.

IV. FORMULAS & EXAMPLES

Labor cost per square: _____ X _____ *squares* = _____

V. CALCULATIONS

530 Concrete Flatwork

Total: $ _____

I. COST DETAIL

530   **Concrete Flatwork**   _____

Subcontract concrete slabs, walks and drives

II. SUPPLIERS & SUBCONTRACTORS

Subcontractor: _____

Contact: _____ Phone: _____

III. NOTES

Obtain a bid from concrete finisher for labor and materials based on square foot of flatwork. This may be included as part of foundation subcontract.

Be sure subcontract does not include work that you intend to perform.

For preliminary cost estimating ask subcontractors for an approximate cost per square foot. Use this figure cautiously! Make sure your final decision is based on a firm bid rather than an estimate.

IV. FORMULAS & EXAMPLES

V. CALCULATIONS

Concrete Cost per square foot: _____ X _____ SF of flatwork = _____

540 Exterior Paint/Log Sealant

Total: $ _____

I. COST DETAIL

A. Subcontract

540a   Subcontract to seal/paint exterior   _____
Subcontract to seal logs and seal or paint exposed trim

B. Materials and Labor Estimate

5401   Exterior Sealant Materials   _____
Stains, sealants, mildicides, insecticides

5402   Exterior Sealant Labor   _____
Labor to apply stains, sealants, mildicides, insecticides

5403   Exterior Paint Materials   _____
Primer, paint for exterior surfaces

5404   Exterior Paint Labor   _____
Labor to apply paint for exterior surfaces

540b   Total   _____

II. SUPPLIERS & SUBCONTRACTORS

Subcontractor: _____
Contact: _____Phone: _____

Materials Supplier: _____
Contact: _____Phone: _____

III. NOTES

Complete Section A if you will be subcontracting the entire job. Complete Section B if you will be performing these jobs yourself or will be purchasing materials for hired labor.

Obtain a bid from painter for labor and materials, or labor only, if you will provide materials.

Be sure subcontract does not include work that you intend to perform.

III. NOTES

Estimate material requirements using the coverages specified by product manufacturers.

IV. FORMULAS & EXAMPLES

_____ *SF of area to cover / square foot coverage per gallon =* _____ *gallons*

V. CALCULATIONS

550 Garage Doors/Openers

Total: $ _____

I. COST DETAIL

5501	**Garage Doors**	_____
	Garage doors not in log home package	
5502	**Garage Door Openers**	_____
5503	**Garage Door Installation**	_____
	Labor to install garage doors/openers	
550	**Total**	_____

II. SUPPLIERS & SUBCONTRACTORS

Supplier: _____

Contact: _____ Phone: _____

Installer: _____

Contact: _____ Phone: _____

III. NOTES

Some log home companies can provide garage doors. However, in some areas it is difficult to find installers for doors not purchased from the installer. It may be easier to obtain door and installation service from a local supplier.

Be sure subcontract does not include work that you intend to perform.

IV. FORMULAS & EXAMPLES

V. CALCULATIONS

560 Rain Gutters

Total: $ _____

I. COST DETAIL

560   **Gutters/ Downspouts** _____

Subcontract to provide gutters, downspouts

II. SUPPLIERS & SUBCONTRACTORS

Subcontractor: _____

Contact: _____Phone: _____

III. NOTES

Obtain bid from gutter supplier. Gutters are often made up on site.

Be sure subcontract does not include work that you intend to perform.

For preliminary cost estimating, ask subcontractors for an approximate cost per linear foot. Use this figure cautiously! Make sure the final figure is based on a firm bid rather than an estimate.

IV. FORMULAS & EXAMPLES

Gutter/downspout cost per linear foot: _____ X _____ LF = _____

V. CALCULATIONS

570 Decks not in package

Total: $ _____

I. COST DETAIL

A. Deck Subcontract

   570a   Subcontract for materials and labor   _____

B. Deck Labor and Materials Estimate

   5701   Deck Materials not in package   _____
Enter total from Deck Materials Worksheet

   5702   Deck Labor not in carpentry contract   _____

   570b   Sub-total of labor and materials   Sub-total _____

II. SUPPLIERS & SUBCONTRACTORS

Materials Supplier: _____
Contact: _____ Phone: _____

Subcontractor: _____
Contact: _____ Phone: _____

III. NOTES

Use the Deck Materials Worksheet to itemize materials that aren't included in the log package.

Be sure to include nails, screws, adhesives and other fasteners.

IV. FORMULAS & EXAMPLES

V. CALCULATIONS

600 Insulation

Total: $＿＿

I. COST DETAIL

A. Subcontract for Insulation

600a   Subcontract for labor and materials
All materials and labor based on blueprints and specifications.   _____

B. Materials and Labor Estimate

6001   Ceiling
Blanket, batt, loose fill, rigid sheet, reflective materials, labor   _____

6002   Wall
Blanket, batt, loose fill, rigid sheet, reflective materials, labor   _____

6003   Floor
Blanket, batt, loose fill, rigid sheet, reflective materials, labor   _____

6004   Foundation
Blanket, batt, loose fill, rigid sheet, reflective materials, labor   _____

600b   Total   _____

II. SUPPLIERS & SUBCONTRACTORS

Subcontractor: _____
Contact: _____ Phone: _____

Materials Supplier: _____
Contact: _____ Phone: _____

III. NOTES

Depending on roof type, roof insulation can be estimated using the area calculated for roof coverings. (See Roofing Materials Not in Package)

Be sure subcontract does not include work that you intend to perform.

For preliminary cost estimating ask subcontractors for an approximate cost per square foot. Use this figure cautiously! Make sure the final figure is based on a firm bid rather than an estimate.

IV. FORMULAS & EXAMPLES

V. CALCULATIONS

610 Drywall

Total: $ _____

I. COST DETAIL

A. Drywall Subcontract

610a   Subcontract   _____
*Enter amount to provide materials and labor to install and
fiinish drywall according to Drywall Specification Sheet.*

B. Drywall Materials and Labor Estimate

6101   Materials   _____
*Total amount for drywall, fasteners, adhesive, tape, joint
compound, corner bead.*

6102   Hang Labor   _____
Labor to install drywall according to specifications.

6103   Finish Labor   _____
Labor to finish drywall according to specifications.

610b   Total   _____

II. SUPPLIERS & SUBCONTRACTORS

Subcontractor: _____
Contact: _____Phone: _____

Materials Supplier: _____
Contact: _____Phone: _____

III. NOTES

*A bid for complete installation and finishing has less risk for error although it
may be slightly more expensive than separate bids.*

*Unless you are familiar with drywall installation in new construction, estimat-
ing can be risky. Ask your drywall material supplier to check your materials
estimates.*

IV. FORMULAS & EXAMPLES

Walls: *Linear feet of framed exterior wall to be covered* = ———————————————

Linear feet of framed interior wall to be covered = ———————————————

Total LF of drywall = ———————————————

(Do not deduct for door or window openings when figuring linear feet)

Total LF Drywall ————— X   *Wall height (ft)* ————— = ————— *SF Drywall wall area*

SF Drywall   *SF*
Wall Area ————— + *Ceiling* ————— + 10%   = ————— *SF Drywall area*

—————*SF Drywall* / 400   = —————*Rolls of tape*

—————*SF Drywall* / 1000 = —————*75 lb container of joint compound*

—————*SF Drywall* / 1000 = —————*5 lb box drywall nails*

—————*SF Drywall* / 150   = —————*Qt tubes of adhesive (if glued)*

For corner bead, total linear feet of outside corners, bulkheads and untrimmed door jambs.

V. CALCULATIONS

620 Interior Finish Materials

Total: $ _____

I. COST DETAIL

620   Interior finish materials not in package   _____
Enter total from Interior Finish Materials Worksheet

II. SUPPLIERS & SUBCONTRACTORS

Finish Materials Supplier: _____

Contact: _____ Phone: _____

III. NOTES

Use the Interior Finish Materials Worksheet to itemize materials that aren't included in the log package.

Be sure to include nails, screws, adhesives and other fasteners.

IV. FORMULAS & EXAMPLES

V. CALCULATIONS

630 Interior Finish Labor

Total: $ _____

I. COST DETAIL

630   **Finish (Trim) Labor**
Subcontract for logs, beams, interior framing, set doors, windows

_____

II. SUPPLIERS & SUBCONTRACTORS

Subcontractor: _____

Contact: _____ Phone: _____

III. NOTES

Obtain a bid from finish carpenter, builder or log builder.

Be sure subcontract does not include work that you intend to perform.

For preliminary cost estimating ask subcontractors for an approximate cost per square foot. Use this figure cautiously! Make sure the final figure is based on a firm bid rather than an estimate.

IV. FORMULAS & EXAMPLES

V. CALCULATIONS

640 Interior Painting/Log Finish

Total: $_____

I. COST DETAIL

A. Subcontract

640a   Subcontract for interior log finish/ painting   _____
*Subcontract to finish logs and paint interior walls and
trim.*

B. Materials and Labor Estimate

6401   Interior Log Finish Materials   _____
Stain, polyurethane, oil

6402   Interior Log Finish Labor   _____
Labor to apply all interior log finish coats

6403   Interior Paint Materials   _____
Primer, paint for interior surfaces

6404   Interior Paint Labor   _____
Labor to apply paint on interior surfaces

640b   Total   _____

II. SUPPLIERS & SUBCONTRACTORS

Subcontractor: _____
Contact: _____ Phone: _____

Materials Supplier: _____
Contact: _____ Phone: _____

III. NOTES

*Complete Section A if you will be subcontracting the entire job. Complete
Section B if you will be performing these jobs yourself or will be purchasing
materials for hired labor.*

*Obtain a bid from painter for labor and materials, or labor only, if you will
provide materials.*

III. NOTES

Be sure subcontract does not include work that you intend to perform.

Estimate material requirements using the coverages specified by product manufacturers.

IV. FORMULAS & EXAMPLES

General formula for calculating paint, stain and finish quantities:

SF of area to cover/ SF coverage per gallon = gallons required

V. CALCULATIONS

650 Ceramic Tile*

Total: $_____

I. COST DETAIL

A. Ceramic Subcontract or Allowance

650a   Subcontract or allowance
Enter amount to provide materials and labor to install and finish Ceramic Tile including backings, underlayments and grout.

_____

B. Ceramic Tile Materials and Labor Estimate

6501   Materials
Total amount for ceramic tile, adhesives, backings and underlayments.

_____

6502   Labor to install
Labor to install ceramic tile including backings, underlayments and grout

_____

650b   Total

_____

II. SUPPLIERS & SUBCONTRACTORS

Subcontractor: _____
Contact: _____Phone: _____

Materials Supplier: _____
Contact: _____Phone: _____

III. NOTES

Unless you are familiar with ceramic tile installation in new construction, estimating can be risky. Ask your material supplier to check your estimates.

Ceramic tile work is often entered as an allowance when preparing an estimate. Identify the approximate cost per square foot for materials and installation and the total number of square feet required. Base allowance on this amount.

Be sure subcontract does not include work that you intend to perform.

IV. FORMULAS & EXAMPLES

Coverage: *Calculate for each type of tile*

Walls: *Square feet of wall area to be covered* =_____

Counters: *Square feet of countertop to be covered* =_____

Floors: *Square feet of floor area to be covered* =_____

Subtotal SF of Ceramic Tile =_____
plus 10% =_____

*Total SF Ceramic tile*_____

Underlayment/Backing: *Calculate for each type of tile*

_____ *SF Tile* / _____ *SF underlayment or* = _____ *Sheets of*
                                      backing per sheet   *underlayment*
                                                           or backing

Adhesives, grout, fasteners: *General formula for calculating material amounts*

_____ *SF Area* / _____ *area per unit or container* = _____ *Quantity of*
                                                               materials

V. CALCULATIONS

670 Cabinets/Vanities/Countertops

Total: $_____

I. COST DETAIL

A. Subcontract for Cabinetry, Countertops

670a   Subcontract for materials and installation   _____
*All materials and labor based on blueprints and
specifications or supplier's diagram*

B. Materials and Labor Estimate

6701	Cabinets	_____
6702	Vanities	_____
6703	Countertops	_____
6704	Installation	_____

Installation of cabinetry, countertops

670b   Total   _____

II. SUPPLIERS & SUBCONTRACTORS

Subcontractor: _____

Contact: _____Phone: _____

Materials Supplier: _____

Contact: _____Phone: _____

III. NOTES

*Cabinetry and countertops are often estimated as an allowance. Obtain the cost
per linear foot for materials and labor from the supplier.*

*Trim or finish carpenters often install cabinetry. You can obtain a separate bid
or have trim carpenter include cabinet and countertop installation with finish
carpentry bid.*

Be sure subcontract does not include work that you intend to perform.

*Use the Cabinetry Worksheet to price cabinets by the unit. Include cabinet
hardware.*

IV. FORMULAS & EXAMPLES

V. CALCULATIONS

680 Vinyl Flooring*

Total: $_____

I. COST DETAIL

A. Vinyl Subcontract or allowance

680a   Subcontract or allowance
*Enter amount to provide materials and labor to install
vinyl including underlayments*

_____

B. Vinyl Materials and Labor Estimate

6801   Materials
Total amount for vinyl, adhesives, and underlayments

_____

6802   Labor to install
*Labor to install vinyl including adhesives and
underlayments*

_____

680b   Total

_____

II. SUPPLIERS & SUBCONTRACTORS

Subcontractor: _____

Contact: _____ Phone: _____

Materials Supplier: _____

Contact: _____ Phone: _____

III. NOTES

*Unless you are familiar with vinyl installation in new construction, estimating
can be risky. Ask your material supplier to check your estimates.*

*Vinyl work is often entered as an allowance when preparing an estimate. Base
allowance on the approximate cost per square foot for materials and installation
and the total number of square feet required.*

Be sure subcontract does not include work that you intend to perform.

IV. FORMULAS & EXAMPLES

Coverage: *Calculate for each type of vinyl (take repeat patterns into account, don't deduct for openings)*

$$\text{Square feet of floor area to be covered} = \underline{\hspace{3cm}}$$
$$\text{plus } 10\% = \underline{\hspace{3cm}}$$

$$\text{Total SF Vinyl} \quad \underline{\hspace{3cm}}$$

Underlayment/Backing: *Calculate for each type of vinyl*

$\underline{\hspace{2cm}}$ SF vinyl / $\underline{\hspace{1cm}}$ SF underlayment or backing per sheet = $\underline{\hspace{1.5cm}}$ Sheets of underlayment or backing

Adhesives, fasteners: *General formula for calculating material amounts*

$\underline{\hspace{2cm}}$ SF Area / $\underline{\hspace{1.5cm}}$ area per unit or container = $\underline{\hspace{2cm}}$ Quantity of materials

V. CALCULATIONS

682 Hardwood Flooring/Floor Finish* | Total: $ _____

I. COST DETAIL

A. Hardwood flooring subcontract or allowance

682a   Subcontract or allowance   _____
*Enter amount to provide materials and labor to install and
finish hardwood including underlayments and finishing*

B. Hardwood Materials and Labor Estimate

6821   Materials   _____
*Total amount for hardwood flooring, adhesives, fasteners
and underlayments.*

6822   Labor to install   _____
*Labor to install hardwood flooring including
underlayments and finishing*

682b   Total   _____

II. SUPPLIERS & SUBCONTRACTORS

Subcontractor: _____
Contact: _____ Phone: _____

Materials Supplier: _____
Contact: _____ Phone: _____

III. NOTES

*Unless you are familiar with hardwood flooring installation in new construc-
tion, estimating can be risky. Ask your material supplier to check your
estimates.*

*Hardwood flooring is often entered as an allowance when preparing an
estimate. Base allowance on the approximate cost per square foot for materials
and installation and the total number of square feet required.*

Be sure subcontract does not include work that you intend to perform.

IV. FORMULAS & EXAMPLES

Coverage: *Calculate for each type of flooring*

Square feet of floor area to be covered = _____

plus 10% = _____

Total SF hardwood _____

Underlayment/Backing: *Calculate for each type of flooring*

_____ SF hardwood / _____ SF underlayment
or backing per sheet = _____ sheets of
underlayment
or backing

Adhesives, fasteners: *General formula for calculating material amounts*

_____ SF Area / _____ area per unit
or container = _____ Material Quantity

V. CALCULATIONS

684 Carpet*

Total: $ _____

I. COST DETAIL

A. Carpet Subcontract or allowance

684a   Subcontract or allowance
Enter amount to provide materials and labor to install carpet including pad   _____

B. Carpet Materials and Labor Estimate

6841   Materials
Total amount for carpet and pads   _____

6842   Labor to install
Labor to install carpet including pads   _____

684b   Total   _____

II. SUPPLIERS & SUBCONTRACTORS

Subcontractor: _____

Contact: _____ Phone: _____

Materials Supplier: _____

Contact: _____ Phone: _____

III. NOTES

Unless you are familiar with carpet installation in new construction, estimating can be risky. Ask your material supplier to check your estimates.

Carpet work is often entered as an allowance when preparing an estimate. Base allowance on the approximate cost per square yard for materials and installation and the total number of square yards required.

Be sure subcontract does not include work that you intend to perform.

IV. FORMULAS & EXAMPLES

Coverage: *Calculate for each type of carpet (take repeat patterns into account, don't deduct for openings)*

Square yards of floor area to be covered   =   _____

plus 10%   =   _____

Total SY carpet _____

V. CALCULATIONS

690 Caulking/Chinking

Total: $____

I. COST DETAIL

A. Subcontract

    690a   Subcontract for caulking/chinking
    Subcontract to caulk or chink logs

B. Materials and Labor Estimate

    6901   Interior caulk/chinking materials
    Materials to caulk/chink interior log walls as per
    manufacturer's specifications or owner

    6902   Interior caulk/chinking labor
    Labor to apply all interior caulking/chinking

    6903   Exterior caulk/chinking materials
    Materials to caulk/chink exterior log walls as per
    manufacturer's specifications or owner

    6904   Exterior caulk/chinking labor
    Labor to apply all interior caulking/chinking

    690b   Total

II. SUPPLIERS & SUBCONTRACTORS

Subcontractor: _____

Contact: _____ Phone: _____

Materials Supplier: _____

Contact: _____Phone: _____

III. NOTES

Complete Section A if you will be subcontracting the entire job. Complete Section B if you will be performing these jobs yourself or will be purchasing materials for hired labor.

Carpenters, builders and painters sometimes can apply caulking or chinking.

Obtain separate bids or have them include in their overall subcontract. Be sure subcontract does not include work that you intend to perform.

Estimate material requirements using the coverages specified by product manufacturers.

IV. FORMULAS & EXAMPLES

General formula for calculating caulk and chinking requirements:

LF of area to cover / linear foot coverage per gallon = gallons required

V. CALCULATIONS

692 Appliances*

Total: $ _____

I. COST DETAIL

692   **Appliances**
    Enter total from Appliance Worksheet

_____

II. SUPPLIERS & SUBCONTRACTORS

Supplier: _____
Contact: _____ Phone: _____

Supplier: _____
Contact: _____ Phone: _____

Supplier: _____
Contact: _____ Phone: _____

Supplier: _____
Contact: _____ Phone: _____

Supplier: _____
Contact: _____ Phone: _____

III. NOTES

Use the Appliance Worksheet to itemize appliances.

Include delivery and installation with appliance prices. Be sure electrician and plumber include necessary plumbing and wiring in their subcontracts.

Appliances are sometimes included as an allowance for estimating purposes. Study catalogs to determine grade of appliances and approximate cost.

IV. FORMULAS & EXAMPLES

V. CALCULATIONS

694 Finish Hardware*

Total: $_____

I. COST DETAIL

694   Finish Hardware
     Enter total from Finish Hardware Worksheet   ──────────

II. SUPPLIERS & SUBCONTRACTORS

Supplier: _____

Contact: _____ Phone: _____

Supplier: _____

Contact: _____ Phone: _____

Supplier: _____

Contact: _____ Phone: _____

Supplier: _____

Contact: _____ Phone: _____

Supplier: _____

Contact: _____ Phone: _____

III. NOTES

Use the Finish Hardware Worksheet to itemize hardware.

Finish hardware is usually installed by the trim or finish carpenter. Be sure hardware installation is included in their bid.

Finish hardware is sometimes included as an allowance for estimating purposes. Study catalogs to determine grade of hardware and approximate cost.

Include cabinet and vanity hardware with cabinetry estimate.

IV. FORMULAS & EXAMPLES

V. CALCULATIONS

696 Fireplaces/Stoves*

Total: $ _____

I. COST DETAIL

696   Subcontract for Fireplaces/ Woodstoves
*Include all materials and labor to install or erect fireplace
or woodstove.*

_____

II. SUPPLIERS & SUBCONTRACTORS

Subcontractor: _____

Contact: _____ **Phone:** _____

Materials Supplier: _____

Contact: _____ **Phone:** _____

III. NOTES

*Fireplaces and woodstoves are often entered as an allowance for estimating
purposes. Discuss styles and costs with suppliers and subcontractors to obtain
a rough estimate.*

*Include artificial stone coverings for zero clearance fireplaces in stone/masonry
estimate.*

Enter masonry fireplaces and chimneys in stone/masonry estimate.

*Include framing labor for zero clearance fireplace units in carpentry labor
subcontract.*

*Include framing materials for zero clearance fireplace with **Framing Materials
not included in Log Package.***

Include zero clearance fireplaces and woodstoves in appliance estimate.

Include plumbing for gas fireplace units in plumbing subcontract.

IV. FORMULAS & EXAMPLES

V. CALCULATIONS

700 Electrical

Total: $_____

I. COST DETAIL

700   **Electrical Subcontract**
Subcontract for wiring home, including rough wiring,
temporary electric service, permit, and installing fixtures

_____

II. SUPPLIERS & SUBCONTRACTORS

Subcontractor: _____

Contract: _____ Phone: _____

III. NOTES

Obtain a bid from electrician using the Electrical Request for Quotation

Be sure subcontract does not include work that you intend to perform.

For preliminary cost estimating ask subcontractors for an approximate cost per square foot. Use this figure cautiously! Make sure the final figure is based on a firm bid rather than an estimate.

IV. FORMULAS & EXAMPLES

V. CALCULATIONS

710 Electrical Fixtures*

Total: $_____

I. COST DETAIL

710   Fixtures
Enter total from Electrical Fixtures Worksheet

_____

II. SUPPLIERS & SUBCONTRACTORS

Supplier: _____
Contact: _____ Phone: _____

Supplier: _____
Contact: _____ Phone: _____

Supplier: _____
Contact: _____ Phone: _____

Supplier: _____
Contact: _____ Phone: _____

Supplier: _____
Contact: _____ Phone: _____

III. NOTES

Use the Electrical Fixtures Worksheet to itemize fixtures.

Electrical fixtures are sometimes included as an allowance for estimating purposes. Study catalogs to determine grade of fixtures and approximate cost.

Be sure to include outside light fixtures, floodlighting, and motion detectors.

IV. FORMULAS & EXAMPLES

V. CALCULATIONS

720 HVAC

Total: $_____

I. COST DETAIL

720   HVAC Subcontract
Subcontract for installing heating, ventilation and air conditioning system including units, ductwork, permits

_____

II. SUPPLIERS & SUBCONTRACTORS

Subcontracter: _____

Contact: _____ **Phone:** _____

III. NOTES

Obtain a bid from HVAC, Plumbing or Electrical subcontractor using the appropriate Request for Quotation.

Be sure subcontract does not include work that you intend to perform.

For preliminary cost estimating, ask subcontractors for an approximate cost per square foot. Use this figure cautiously! Make sure the final figure is based on a firm bid rather than an estimate.

Plumber may include hot water heat in plumbing subcontract.

Electrician may include baseboard electric heat in electrical subcontract.

IV. FORMULAS & EXAMPLES

V. CALCULATIONS

730 Plumbing

| Total: $ _____ |

I. COST DETAIL

730 **Plumbing Subcontract**
*Subcontract for plumbing home, including rough in,
permit, and installing fixtures*

_____

II. SUPPLIERS & SUBCONTRACTORS

Plumbing Subcontractor: _____

Contact: _____ **Phone:** _____

III. NOTES

Obtain a bid from plumber using the Plumbing Request for Quotation

Be sure subcontract does not include work that you intend to perform.

*For preliminary cost estimating ask subcontractors for an approximate cost per
square foot. Use this figure cautiously! Make sure the final estimate includes a
firm bid rather than an estimate.*

Plumber may include gas line installation if specified.

IV. FORMULAS & EXAMPLES

V. CALCULATIONS

740 Telephone Wiring

Total: $ _____

I. COST DETAIL

740   Telephone Wiring Subcontract   _____
*Subcontract for installing telephone wiring including
wires and jacks from service head.*

II. SUPPLIERS & SUBCONTRACTORS

Subcontractor: _____

Contact: _____ Phone: _____

III. NOTES

Obtain a bid from installer if not included in electrical subcontract.

Be sure subcontract does not include work that you intend to perform.

*For preliminary cost estimating, ask subcontractors for an approximate cost per
square foot. Use this figure cautiously! Make sure the final figures is based on
a firm bid rather than an estimate.*

IV. FORMULAS & EXAMPLES

V. CALCULATIONS

750 TV/Computer Prewire

Total: $_____

I. COST DETAIL

750   TV/ Computer Pre- Wiring Subcontract
   Subcontract for installing TV/computer wiring from
   service head including wire and jacks

_____

II. SUPPLIERS & SUBCONTRACTORS

Subcontractor: _____

Contact: _____   Phone: _____

III. NOTES

Obtain a bid from installer if not included in electrical subcontract.

Be sure subcontract does not include work that you intend to perform.

For preliminary cost estimating, ask subcontractors for an approximate cost per square foot. Use this figure cautiously! Make sure the final figure is based on a firm bid rather than an estimate.

IV. FORMULAS & EXAMPLES

V. CALCULATIONS

800 Final Grade

Total: $ _____

I. COST DETAIL

8001   **Final grade foundation**   _____
Final grade foundation including restoring topsoil

8002   **Equipment Pickup/Delivery**   _____
Deliver/pickup equipment

800   **Total**   _____

II. SUPPLIERS & SUBCONTRACTORS

Foundation Subcontractor: _____
Contact: _____ **Phone:** _____

III. NOTES

Excavation work is usually priced by the hour for equipment and operator. Ask for an hourly rate and estimate time required to do work. If subcontracting excavation, have excavator include backfill, rough grading and finish grading in their subcontract.

Excavators usually charge for equipment delivery and pick-up. Be sure to include these charges when estimating. If subcontracting, have excavator include equipment moving charges.

IV. FORMULAS & EXAMPLES

_____ *hours* @ _____ *per hour* = _____

V. CALCULATIONS

810 Rake, Straw, Seed*

Total: $ _____

I. COST DETAIL

A. Subcontract for Raking, Straw and Seeding

810a   Subcontract for labor and materials
All materials and labor to rake surface, seed and spread straw

_____

B. Materials and Labor Estimate

8101   Rake house area by hand or machine   _____
Cost to rake bare soil and prepare surface for seeding

8102   Straw   _____
Spread straw bales over seeded area, includes straw and labor to spread

8103   Seed   _____
Seed prepared area, includes seed and application

810b   Total   _____

II. SUPPLIERS & SUBCONTRACTORS

Subcontractor: _____

Contact: _____ Phone: _____

Straw Supplier: _____

Contact: _____ Phone: _____

Seed Supplier: _____

Contact: _____ Phone: _____

III. NOTES

Complete Section A if you will be subcontracting the entire job. Complete Section B if you will be performing these jobs yourself or will be purchasing materials for hired labor.

This is often entered as an allowance for estimating purposes. Obtain bid from landscaper or nursery.

IV. FORMULAS & EXAMPLES

V. CALCULATIONS

820 Landscape*

Total: $_____

I. COST DETAIL

820   **Subcontract for labor and materials**   _____
*All materials and labor to landscape grounds according to
plot plan or landscaping plan*

II. SUPPLIERS & SUBCONTRACTORS

Landscape Subcontractor: _____
Contact: _____Phone: _____

III. NOTES

*This is often entered as an allowance for estimating purposes. Obtain bid
from landscaper or nursery.*

IV. FORMULAS & EXAMPLES

V. CALCULATIONS

830 Drives, Walks, Patios*

Total: $ _____

I. COST DETAIL

830   Subcontract for labor and materials   _____
*Materials & labor for entrance road, walks, patios,
including drainage pipes, railings, asphalt or concrete,
if required*

II. SUPPLIERS & SUBCONTRACTORS

Subcontractor: _____

Contact: _____ Phone: _____

III. NOTES

*This is often entered as an allowance for estimating purposes. Obtain bid from
excavator or concrete subcontractor.*

IV. FORMULAS & EXAMPLES

V. CALCULATIONS

840 Retaining Walls*

Total: $_____

I. COST DETAIL

840   **Subcontract for labor and materials**
*Materials & labor for retaining walls specified on
blueprints or required by excavation*

_____

II. SUPPLIERS & SUBCONTRACTORS

Subcontractor: _____

Contact: _____ Phone: _____

III. NOTES

*This is often entered as an allowance for estimating purposes. Obtain bid from
foundation subcontractor, landscaper or nursery.*

IV. FORMULAS & EXAMPLES

V. CALCULATIONS

850 Trash Removal, Clean-up

Total: $_____

I. COST DETAIL

850   Subcontract for labor and materials
   *Materials & labor for removing trash and construction
   rubble including hauling charges and landfill fees*

_____

II. SUPPLIERS & SUBCONTRACTORS

Subcontractor: _____
Contact: _____ Phone: _____

III. NOTES

*This is often entered as an allowance for estimating purposes. Obtain bid from
subcontractor.*

IV. FORMULAS & EXAMPLES

V. CALCULATIONS

900 Contingency

Total: $ _____

I. COST DETAIL

900   Contingency

Use a factor of 5-10% of subtotaled construction costs as a contingency. A lower percentage should be satisfactory if most of the costs in the cost estimate summary are included in signed bids that are based on accurate specifications. Use a larger contingency when the itemized costs are based on estimates rather than bids. As an alternative, add a contingency to each of the cost details, varying the amount of the contingency according to your confidence in the accuracy of the detail cost.

II. SUPPLIERS & SUBCONTRACTORS

III. NOTES

IV. FORMULAS & EXAMPLES

_____ *Construction costs based on specific bids*   X   5%   =   _____ *Contingency*

_____ *Construction costs based on estimates*   X   10%   =   _____ *Contingency*

V. CALCULATIONS

920 Financial Costs

Total: $ _____

I. COST DETAIL

920   Estimated Loan Interest   _____

II. SUPPLIERS & SUBCONTRACTORS

Lender: _____

Contact: _____ Phone: _____

III. NOTES

Obtain an estimate from the loan company. Be sure to include closing costs.

Calculations below assume an even distribution of contruction loan proceeds beginning at "0" (No land draw).

IV. FORMULAS & EXAMPLES

To calculate approximate loan interest on a 12-month loan:

$$\frac{Construction\ Loan\ Amount \quad X \quad Annual\ Interest\ Rate}{2} = \$ _____$$

(For six-month loan, divide by 4 instead of 2)

V. CALCULATIONS

Log Home Cost Summary Sheet

ITEM NUMBER	DESCRIPTION	COMMENTS	BID/ ESTIMATE
100	Lot Cost	Land, closing costs,taxes, easements	$
200	Survey	Boundary, topography, site plan, septic, field location, house layout, wall check, house location	$
210	Plans	All plans, architectural fees, engineering fees not included with kit	$
220	Permits/Fees	Building permit, driveway entrance fee, impact fees, etc. Contact local building authority for complete list	$
230	Sewer/Septic*	Perk test, install septic system, install line & hook up to house	$
240	Water Connection/Well*	Drill well, install pump & tank, hook up to house, test water if required	$
250	Electric Service*	Install power line, transformer, set meter & connect service to house electric panel; Contact local power company for estimate	$
260	Natural Gas/ Propane*	Install natural gas line or set propane tank	$
270	Portable Toilet	Rental for construction period	$
280	Storage Van	Rental for construction period	$
300	Clearing/Site Preparation*	Clear trees & underbrush, cut wood into firewood lengths, stack, remove or bury stumps	$
310	Lot Layout	Surveyor or contractor to mark house corners & set offset stakes for digging foundation	$
320	Excavating*	Dig foundation, separate topsoil	$
330	Footings	Dig footings, install steel, pour concrete	$
340	Foundation	Erect foundation walls, install drain tile around foundation, apply waterproofing	$

Often entered as an allowance, obtain estimate to be sure figures are realistic

350	Steel	Furnish & install any special steel reinforcement or beams required	$
360	Termite Treatment	Treat foundation, furnish certificate & warranty	$
370	Backfill/Rough Grading	Backfill around foundation & smooth to within six inches of final grade	$
380	Gravel Fill	Furnish & install, if required	$
400	Log Package, including delivery	Complete kit cost, including delivery	$
410	Unloading Logs inc. forklift, labor	Forklift rental, labor to unload & stack kit (may be included with construction contract)	$
415	Crane, heavy equip- ment rental	Crane rental for log, beam installation if required, other heavy equipment	$
420	Windows/Doors not in pkg	Delivered price	$
430	Framing Materials not in pkg	Delivered price for framing not in kit	$
440	Logwork/Framing Labor	Cost to erect all or part of kit	$
500	Masonry/Stone	Material & labor for stone veneer on foundation, retaining walls, fireplace chimneys	$
510	Roofing Material not in pkg	Shingles, rafters, beams not in kit	$
520	Roofing Labor	Shingling including drip edge & ridge vent	$
530	Concrete Flatwork	Basement, garage, porch floor slabs	$
540	Exterior Paint/Log Sealant	Materials & labor	$

550	Garage Doors/Openers	Materials & installation labor	$
560	Rain Gutters	Splashblocks for downspouts & outside water spigots	$
570	Decks not in pkg	Materials & labor	$
600	Insulation	Materials & labor for ceiling, roof, subfloor or foundation, framed wall insulation, check local building code requirements.	$
610	Drywall	Furnish, install, finish joints	$
620	Interior Finish Material	Baseboards, closet shelves, rods, crown & specialty mouldings, interior doors, jambs, trim, interior window trim, stairs	$
630	Interior Finish Labor	Install interior finish materials, trim, hardware	$
640	Interior Painting/Log Finish	Materials & labor, including sanding, filling nail holes	$
650	Ceramic Tile*	Materials & labor, include underlayment, adhesives, grout	$
670	Cabinets/Vanities/ Countertops	Kitchen, bath, laundry/utility room cabinets, vanities, medicine cabinets	$
680	Vinyl Flooring*	Materials & installation, include underlayment, adhesives	$
682	Hardwood Flooring /inc. floor finish*	Materials & labor, flooring, underlayment, sand, seal, finish	$
684	Carpet*	Materials & labor	$
690	Caulking/Chinking	Materials & labor	$
692	Appliances*	Refrigerator, range, microwave, cook-top, dishwasher, disposal, washer, dryer	$

Often entered as an allowance, obtain estimate to be sure figures are realistic

Log Home Cost Summary Sheet continued

694	Finish Hardware*	Door locksets, hinges, door stops, towel bars, toilet paper holders,	$
696	Fireplaces/Stoves*	Material & installation, fireplace, chimney, hearth, mantel, cap	$
700	Electrical	Install service panel, rough wiring, switches, plugs, covers, hook up appliances, HVAC, hot water heater, smoke detectors, cable TV, telephone	$
710	Electrical Fixtures*	Material & labor for lighting fixtures, flood lights, motion sensors	$
720	HVAC	Materials & labor for heating, ventilation & air conditioning, include bathroom, dryer vents, humidifiers, dehumidifiers, air cleaners	$
730	Plumbing	Materials & labor for rough plumbing, hot water heaters, tubs, showers, toilets, bidets, saunas, steam rooms, hook up icemaker, disposal, sump pump	$
740	Telephone Wiring	If separate from electric	$
750	TV/Computer Pre-wire	If separate from electric	$
800	Final Grade	Final grade, replace topsoil	$
810	Rake, Straw, Seed*	Materials & labor	$
820	Landscape*	Materials & labor as per landscape plan	$
830	Drives, Walks, Patios*	Materials & labor to clear, grade, gravel & finish entrance road or drive, including, install drainage pipes, railings, asphalt or concrete if required	$
840	Retaining Walls*	Materials & labor	$
850	Trash Removal, Clean-up	Removal of construction debris, include hauling & dumping fees	$

Often entered as an allowance, obtain estimate to be sure figures are realistic

	SUBTOTAL		$
900	Contingency	Itemize contingencies or add minimum of 5% of subtotal for unexpected expenses	$
920	Financial Costs	Obtain estimate from lender	$
	TOTAL		$

III Worksheets and Schedules

Log Homes Made Easy™
Project Planner

III. Using Worksheets and Schedules

This section contains supplemental **Worksheets and Schedules**. Some of the worksheets support Cost Detail Sheets in Section II. Others are provided for you to use as references. Schedules are for information that is important for you or your subcontractors during the construction of your home. Think of a schedule as a "What goes where" worksheet. The **Window** and **Door Schedules** are examples. They contain information about which window and door units go where in your home. They also indicate unit sizes, the size openings necessary and price. Your blueprint set may also contain window and door schedules. Be sure to verify these against your materials list to make sure that item counts, sizes, types and door swings agree with the blueprints. Both window and door specifications change frequently during the design process so it's important to make sure that the schedules contain the most recent information.

The **Room Finish Schedule** is especially important. It contains information about the floors, walls and ceilings of each room of your log home. I suggest completing the Room Finish Schedule before you complete your Requests For Quotations to make sure that your Requests are consistent with how you want each room finished. Post copies of the Room Finish Schedule around the house during construction. It provides useful information for carpenters, drywall hangers and painters. For example, interior doors may be set to slightly different heights depending on the floor covering. By knowing which areas are carpeted and which receive hardwood, the carpenter can leave the appropriate clearance when setting door units. You can also note which rooms receive wallpaper so that the walls of those rooms can be prepared properly.

You can also use the worksheets for obtaining material price quotes or ordering materials. For example, if you choose not to purchase windows as part of your log home package, you can use the Window Worksheet to obtain an estimate from several suppliers. You can then use the same worksheet as an order form.

Window Worksheet

Windows

Ref #	Qty	Manufacturer	Description	Mfr ID	Unit Cost	Total Cost
						$
						$
						$
						$
						$
						$
						$
						$
						$
						$
						$
						$
						$
						$
						$
						$
						$
						$
						$
						$
						$
						$
						$
						$
						$
					Subtotal:	$
					Sales Tax:	$
					Delivery:	$
					Total:	$

Door Worksheet

Doors

Page ____ of _____

Ref #	Qty	Manufacturer	Description	Mfr ID	Unit Cost	Total Cost
						$
						$
						$
						$
						$
						$
						$
						$
						$
						$
						$
						$
						$
						$
						$
						$
						$
						$
						$
						$
						$
						$
						$
						$
					Subtotal:	$
					Sales Tax:	$
					Delivery:	$
					Total:	$

Framing Materials Worksheet

Page ____ of ____

Ref #	Item	T	W	L	Qty	Unit Cost	Total Cost
							$
							$
							$
							$
							$
							$
							$
							$
							$
							$
							$
							$
							$
							$
							$
							$
							$
							$
							$
							$
							$
							$
							$
							$
						Subtotal:	$
						Sales Tax:	$
						Delivery:	$
						Total:	$

Roof Materials Worksheet

Page _____ of _____

Item	T	W	L	Qty	Unit Cost	Total Cost
						$
						$
						$
						$
						$
						$
						$
						$
						$
						$
						$
						$
						$
						$
						$
						$
						$
						$
						$
						$
						$
						$
						$
						$
						$
					Subtotal:	$
					Sales Tax:	$
					Delivery:	$
					Total:	$

Deck Materials Worksheet

Page ____ of _____

Item	T	W	L	Qty	Unit Cost	Total Cost
						$
						$
						$
						$
						$
						$
						$
						$
						$
						$
						$
						$
						$
						$
						$
						$
						$
						$
						$
						$
						$
						$
						$
						$
					Subtotal:	$
					Sales Tax:	$
					Delivery:	$
					Total:	$

Interior Finish Materials Worksheet

Page _____ of _____

Item	T	W	L	Qty	Unit Cost	Total Cost
						$
						$
						$
						$
						$
						$
						$
						$
						$
						$
						$
						$
						$
						$
						$
						$
						$
						$
						$
						$
						$
						$
						$
						$
						$
					Subtotal:	$
					Sales Tax:	$
					Delivery:	$
					Total:	$

Cabinetry Materials Worksheet

Page _____ of _____

Item/Unit #	T	W	L	Qty	Unit Cost	Total Cost
						$
						$
						$
						$
						$
						$
						$
						$
						$
						$
						$
						$
						$
						$
						$
						$
						$
						$
						$
						$
						$
						$
						$
						$
					Subtotal:	$
					Sales Tax:	$
					Delivery:	$
					Total:	$

Appliance Worksheet

Page _____ of _____

Item/Unit #	Manufacturer	Model #	Color	Supplier	Total Cost
Refrigerator					$
Range/Oven					$
Cooktop					$
Dishwasher					$
Microwave					$
Disposal					$
Compactor					$
Instant Hot Water					$
Woodstove					$
Fireplace					$
Washer					$
Dryer					$
					$
				Subtotal:	$
				Sales Tax:	$
				Delivery:	$
				Total:	$

Finish Hardware Worksheet

Page _____ of _____

Item/Unit #	Manufacturer/ Supplier	Style/Model/ Size	Color/ Finish	Qty	Unit Cost	Total Cost
Front Door lockset						$
Privacy locksets						$
Passage locksets						$
Doorstops						$
Deadbolts						$
Towel bars						$
Toilet paper holders						$
Closet rod holders						$
Shelf brackets						$
Mirrors						$
Hinge sets						$
						$
					Subtotal:	$
					Sales Tax:	$
					Delivery:	$
					Total:	$

Electrical Fixtures Worksheet

Page _____ of _____

Room	Fixture	Manufacturer/ Model	Color	Supplier	Total Cost
					$
					$
					$
					$
					$
					$
					$
					$
					$
					$
					$
					$
				Subtotal:	$
				Sales Tax:	$
				Delivery:	$
				Total:	$

Door Schedule

ID	Mfr/Number	Size	Swing	Log Opening	Mfr RO	Qty	Unit Price	Total Price

Window Schedule

Blueprint ID	Manufacturer Number	Log Opening Dimensions	Mfr RO	Qty	Unit Price	Total Price

Room Finish Schedule

Room ID	Wall				Ceiling	Floor
Entry/Foyer						
Living/Great Room						
Dining Room						
Kitchen						
Family Room						
Master Bedroom						

Room Finish Schedule continued

Room ID	Wall	Ceiling	Floor
Bedroom #2			
Bedroom #3			
Bedroom #4			
Bedroom #5			
Master Bath			
Bath #2			

Room Finish Schedule continued

Room ID	Wall	Ceiling	Floor
Bath #3			
Powder Room			
Office/Den #1			
Office/Den #2			
Hall #1			
Hall #2			

© 2001 Jim Cooper

Room Finish Schedule continued

Room ID	Wall	Ceiling	Floor
Garage			

Preparing Your Construction Calendar

Summary

Make at least three copies of the blank Calendar pages, keeping the originals for future needs. Lay out your entire Construction Calendar on one set of forms using the tips and instructions below, marking each page "Preliminary Calendar."

Duplicate the first week of your Calendar and designate it as a "Working Calendar". At the end of the first week, review what has been accomplished from your Working Calendar. Transfer items that weren't completed to a new "Second Week" Sheet and designate it as "Working". Complete the second week working calendar by referring to your Preliminary Calendar.

At the end of the second week, review what has been accomplished and transfer any uncompleted activities to a blank "Third Week" Calendar Sheet designated as "Working". Once previous uncompleted activities have been added, refer to your Preliminary Calendar to complete the rest of the week.

Using the Calendar

The Construction Calendar is laid out according to a generalized "critical path" for construction activity. The activity at the top of each page must generally precede the items listed further down. Review the Construction Calendar sequence with your subs before construction begins to see if there are any activities that need to be adjusted in the construction sequence. For example, if you are building a solid masonry fireplace, the fireplace footing is dug along with the house footings and the base is usually prepared as the foundation is being installed. Block or stonework either precedes or follows log work, depending on whether the fireplace is located on an outside wall or in the interior of the house. If your fireplace is "zero-clearance," that is a woodburning or gas fireplace unit set into a framed chimney that is covered with artificial stone, the construction sequence is different. Unless you are familiar with home building, don't try to figure out the appropriate construction sequence yourself. Instead ask your subcontractors. They can point out the best place in the construction sequence for their activity.

What to note on the Calendar

- When to place materials orders to have them delivered on time
- When to confirm materials order
- When to notify subs that you will be ready for them
- Specific activities, blocking out the estimated time required (obtain an estimate of the time required from the sub)
- When to schedule inspections
- Scheduled inspections
- Completed Inspections

Why two Calendars?

Because construction never proceeds according to your original intentions, I suggest preparing two calendars: a Preliminary Calendar for the entire project, and a Working Calendar one to two weeks in advance as construction progresses. Delays due to weather, material shortages and subcontractors will require you to modify your schedule often. Many times you cannot "work around" an activity but must simply back everything up until it is done. Your Preliminary Calendar provides a reference to keep you on track while your working calendar reflects the reality of construction.

Working With Subcontractors

Notifying subs

When you inform subs you have selected them for your project, tell them when you anticipate starting and find out how much advance notice they need to work you into their schedule. Many subs (especially good ones) have regular clients who keep them busy at certain times. Don't expect a sub to drop work for a regular builder client and rush to your job at your call. Be sure to ask about the general time period when you will need the sub. A sub who requires a month's advance notice in the spring, may only need two or three days in the fall. Note the amount of advance notice required on your subcontract. As you prepare your preliminary calendar, enter the time to notify the sub in the appropriate place. For example, if you anticipate plumbing work starting in the beginning of Week 7 and the plumber says he will need a week's notice, enter a note to call the plumber at the beginning of Week 6.

As work progresses, keep subs informed of changes in your schedule. If you have notified the electrician you will be ready at the beginning of Week 8 and by Week 6 you realize that you won't be finished with interior framing, notify the electrician of the delay and when you anticipate needing him. Don't let subs arrive on your jobsite expecting to go to work when the site isn't ready for them. You may find yourself bumped to the bottom of their schedule.

Ordering and confirming materials orders

Note the amount of advance notice required to arrange a delivery from major suppliers. Enter the date you need the delivery and the date to call and place your order. For example, if you know that you will be ready to install carpeting in Week 10 and the supplier says they will need two weeks advance notice in order to take final measurements and get your materials, note the day you want carpeting on your jobsite and then make a note two weeks prior to contact the carpet supplier.

Never have subs or installers arrive on your jobsite when the materials they need to do their work won't be available. Subs get paid only for work accomplished. If they block time in their schedule for your job and then arrive to find materials missing, they must either move to another job or go a day without pay. If they start another job, they will probably not return to yours until that one is finished or can be interrupted. Careful coordination is critical to keeping a project on schedule and on budget.

Paying Subs—Lien Waivers

Every subcontractor will have a payment policy. For some it will be payment in full on completion or from an invoice sent when work is completed. Others may require an initial payment before work begins, a second or "progress" payment when rough-in or preliminary work has been completed, and a final payment when all work is done. Understand the sub's payment policy before work begins.

Keep any advance payments small. Control as much of the sub's money as possible until work is completed. Be sure to check the references of any sub requesting an advance payment. Subsidizing a struggling subcontractor is risky business.

Make sure criteria are clearly stated for progress payments. Pay only after the criteria have been met.

Hold final payment until any necessary inspections have been completed. If possible, also wait until the next sub in the schedule arrives. This way, if the incoming sub finds problems that must be corrected before they can begin, you can call the previous sub back. Once you have made final payment, you may find it difficult to get a sub to return to your jobsite on short notice.

In most states, Mechanics Lien Laws allow subcontractors to file a lien against property where they have contributed work for which they have not been paid. The lien is recorded against the property and must be resolved in order to complete the permanent mortgage. Occasionally during construction, there is disagreement between a sub and homeowner about whether work is covered in the price of a subcontract, especially when the work involves changes made during construction. Sometimes a homeowner thinks that by simply refusing payment, they can settle the argument. Mechanics Lien Laws make this a risky and even costly strategy.

To avoid such risks, have a sub sign a **Lien Waiver** when receiving final payment. By signing the waiver, the sub acknowledges that he has been paid for all work. You can find a lien waiver form in Section V.

Using Change Orders

Few log homes are built without some modifications made during construction. These may be as slight as shifting a window location or as large as adding doors, windows, decks or increasing the size of the home. No matter how large or small the change, it's important to understand how subcontractors handle changes.

Most subs' bids are based on blueprints and specifications provided in the Request for Quotation. Any deviation or modification of these constitutes a change and may result in extra charges. Most subs have Change Order forms to handle on site changes. On the Change Order, they will note the work to be done and the estimated cost (often, a sub will not provide a firm price until the change work is completed). Sometimes subs simply perform the additional work and then submit a change order or submit the change order with their final invoice. In a log home construction project, such changes can add up to thousands or tens of thousands of extra charges. Unless these are expected and planned for, they can be devastating to a budget. Before beginning work, make sure the sub understands that you will only pay for changes for which there is a signed change order. If the sub doesn't have a Change Order form, use the one in Section V. Always be sure that you and the sub have agreed, in writing, to any deviation from the original bid, and the cost of the deviation, before the sub performs any actual labor.

Inspections

In most areas of the country, your construction project will be subject to inspection from the local building code enforcement authority. In addition, your lender usually requires periodic inspections before releasing money from construction loan funds. Record scheduled inspections on your construction calendar.

In some cases, subcontractors may schedule inspections directly. This often works better because the sub knows whom to call and when. Discuss any inspection requirements with the sub and clarify who will be ordering the inspection. In areas with a lot of building activity, it may be necessary to schedule inspections several days in advance. To avoid interrupting work, note the date to schedule inspections as well as the inspection itself on your Construction Calendar.

Project Calendar -- Week 1

Project Name: _____

Start Date: _____   Est. Completion Date: _____

ITEM	MONDAY	TUESDAY	WEDNESDAY	THURSDAY	FRIDAY
Pre-Construction					
Road/Driveway					
Well					
Septic System					
Site Preparation					
Excavation					
Foundation					
Insect Treatment					
Slab					
Framing					
Roofing					
HVAC					
Plumbing					
Electric					
Insulation					
Drywall					
Painting					
Trim					
Appliances					
Cabinets					
Floor Coverings					
Gutters					
Landscaping					

Project Calendar-- Week 2

Project Name: _____

Start Date: _____   Est. Completion Date: _____

ITEM	MONDAY	TUESDAY	WEDNESDAY	THURSDAY	FRIDAY
Pre-Construction					
Road/Driveway					
Well					
Septic System					
Site Preparation					
Excavation					
Foundation					
Insect Treatment					
Slab					
Framing					
Roofing					
HVAC					
Plumbing					
Electric					
Insulation					
Drywall					
Painting					
Trim					
Appliances					
Cabinets					
Floor Coverings					
Gutters					
Landscaping					

Project Calendar— Week 3

Project Name: _____

Start Date: _____   Est. Completion Date: _____

ITEM	MONDAY	TUESDAY	WEDNESDAY	THURSDAY	FRIDAY
Pre-Construction					
Road/Driveway					
Well					
Septic System					
Site Preparation					
Excavation					
Foundation					
Insect Treatment					
Slab					
Framing					
Roofing					
HVAC					
Plumbing					
Electric					
Insulation					
Drywall					
Painting					
Trim					
Appliances					
Cabinets					
Floor Coverings					
Gutters					
Landscaping					

Project Calendar— Week 4

Project Name: _____

Start Date: _____   Est. Completion Date: _____

ITEM	MONDAY	TUESDAY	WEDNESDAY	THURSDAY	FRIDAY
Pre-Construction					
Road / Driveway					
Well					
Septic System					
Site Preparation					
Excavation					
Foundation					
Insect Treatment					
Slab					
Framing					
Roofing					
HVAC					
Plumbing					
Electric					
Insulation					
Drywall					
Painting					
Trim					
Appliances					
Cabinets					
Floor Coverings					
Gutters					
Landscaping					

Project Calendar-- Week 5

Project Name: _____   Start Date: _____   Est. Completion Date: _____

ITEM	MONDAY	TUESDAY	WEDNESDAY	THURSDAY	FRIDAY
Pre-Construction					
Road/Driveway					
Well					
Septic System					
Site Preparation					
Excavation					
Foundation					
Insect Treatment					
Slab					
Framing					
Roofing					
HVAC					
Plumbing					
Electric					
Insulation					
Drywall					
Painting					
Trim					
Appliances					
Cabinets					
Floor Coverings					
Gutters					
Landscaping					

Project Calendar-- Week 6

Project Name: _____

Start Date: _____   Est. Completion Date: _____

ITEM	MONDAY	TUESDAY	WEDNESDAY	THURSDAY	FRIDAY
Pre-Construction					
Road/Driveway					
Well					
Septic System					
Site Preparation					
Excavation					
Foundation					
Insect Treatment					
Slab					
Framing					
Roofing					
HVAC					
Plumbing					
Electric					
Insulation					
Drywall					
Painting					
Trim					
Appliances					
Cabinets					
Floor Coverings					
Gutters					
Landscaping					

Project Calendar-- Week 7

Project Name: _____   Start Date: _____   Est. Completion Date: _____

ITEM	MONDAY	TUESDAY	WEDNESDAY	THURSDAY	FRIDAY
Pre-Construction					
Road/Driveway					
Well					
Septic System					
Site Preparation					
Excavation					
Foundation					
Insect Treatment					
Slab					
Framing					
Roofing					
HVAC					
Plumbing					
Electric					
Insulation					
Drywall					
Painting					
Trim					
Appliances					
Cabinets					
Floor Coverings					
Gutters					
Landscaping					

Project Calendar-- Week 8

Project Name: _____

Start Date: _____   Est. Completion Date: _____

ITEM	MONDAY	TUESDAY	WEDNESDAY	THURSDAY	FRIDAY
Pre-Construction					
Road/Driveway					
Well					
Septic System					
Site Preparation					
Excavation					
Foundation					
Insect Treatment					
Slab					
Framing					
Roofing					
HVAC					
Plumbing					
Electric					
Insulation					
Drywall					
Painting					
Trim					
Appliances					
Cabinets					
Floor Coverings					
Gutters					
Landscaping					

Project Calendar

Project Calendar-- Week 9

Project Name: _____ Start Date: _____ Est. Completion Date: _____

ITEM	MONDAY	TUESDAY	WEDNESDAY	THURSDAY	FRIDAY
Pre-Construction					
Road/Driveway					
Well					
Septic System					
Site Preparation					
Excavation					
Foundation					
Insect Treatment					
Slab					
Framing					
Roofing					
HVAC					
Plumbing					
Electric					
Insulation					
Drywall					
Painting					
Trim					
Appliances					
Cabinets					
Floor Coverings					
Gutters					
Landscaping					

© 2001 Jim Cooper

Project Calendar-- Week 10

Project Name: _____

Start Date: _____

Est. Completion Date: _____

ITEM	MONDAY	TUESDAY	WEDNESDAY	THURSDAY	FRIDAY
Pre-Construction					
Road/Driveway					
Well					
Septic System					
Site Preparation					
Excavation					
Foundation					
Insect Treatment					
Slab					
Framing					
Roofing					
HVAC					
Plumbing					
Electric					
Insulation					
Drywall					
Painting					
Trim					
Appliances					
Cabinets					
Floor Coverings					
Gutters					
Landscaping					

Project Calendar-- Week 11

Project Name: _____

Start Date: _____   Est. Completion Date: _____

ITEM	MONDAY	TUESDAY	WEDNESDAY	THURSDAY	FRIDAY
Pre-Construction					
Road/Driveway					
Well					
Septic System					
Site Preparation					
Excavation					
Foundation					
Insect Treatment					
Slab					
Framing					
Roofing					
HVAC					
Plumbing					
Electric					
Insulation					
Drywall					
Painting					
Trim					
Appliances					
Cabinets					
Floor Coverings					
Gutters					
Landscaping					

Project Calendar-- Week 12

Project Name: _____

Start Date: _____   Est. Completion Date: _____

ITEM	MONDAY	TUESDAY	WEDNESDAY	THURSDAY	FRIDAY
Pre-Construction					
Road/Driveway					
Well					
Septic System					
Site Preparation					
Excavation					
Foundation					
Insect Treatment					
Slab					
Framing					
Roofing					
HVAC					
Plumbing					
Electric					
Insulation					
Drywall					
Painting					
Trim					
Appliances					
Cabinets					
Floor Coverings					
Gutters					
Landscaping					

Project Calendar— Week 13

Project Name: _____ Start Date: _____ Est. Completion Date: _____

ITEM	MONDAY	TUESDAY	WEDNESDAY	THURSDAY	FRIDAY
Pre-Construction					
Road/Driveway					
Well					
Septic System					
Site Preparation					
Excavation					
Foundation					
Insect Treatment					
Slab					
Framing					
Roofing					
HVAC					
Plumbing					
Electric					
Insulation					
Drywall					
Painting					
Trim					
Appliances					
Cabinets					
Floor Coverings					
Gutters					
Landscaping					

Project Calendar-- Week 14

Project Name: _____

Start Date: _____   Est. Completion Date: _____

ITEM	MONDAY	TUESDAY	WEDNESDAY	THURSDAY	FRIDAY
Pre-Construction					
Road/Driveway					
Well					
Septic System					
Site Preparation					
Excavation					
Foundation					
Insect Treatment					
Slab					
Framing					
Roofing					
HVAC					
Plumbing					
Electric					
Insulation					
Drywall					
Painting					
Trim					
Appliances					
Cabinets					
Floor Coverings					
Gutters					
Landscaping					

Project Calendar— Week

Project Name: _____

Start Date: _____   Est. Completion Date: _____

ITEM	MONDAY	TUESDAY	WEDNESDAY	THURSDAY	FRIDAY
Pre-Construction					
Road/Driveway					
Well					
Septic System					
Site Preparation					
Excavation					
Foundation					
Insect Treatment					
Slab					
Framing					
Roofing					
HVAC					
Plumbing					
Electric					
Insulation					
Drywall					
Painting					
Trim					
Appliances					
Cabinets					
Floor Coverings					
Gutters					
Landscaping					

V Miscellaneous Forms and Reference

Miscellaneous Forms and References

This section contains forms and information you may find useful as you plan or build your log home. Some of the items are also explained or referenced in other sections.

Record daily activities during construction with the **Daily Site Visit Report**. Note current activity and things you must do or materials you must order for future activity. A record of daily activity can be useful if disputes arise concerning how long an activity took or the condition of the jobsite.

Use the **Subcontractor/Supplier Record** for recording business and contact information for potential subcontractors and suppliers. Be sure to obtain Certificates of Insurance on all subs who work on your project.

Use the **Change Order Form** to track changes to your original plans or specifications as construction progresses. Number and complete the form before any changes or "extra" work is started. Make sure your subcontractors understand that you will only pay additional charges for items covered by a written change order. Changes to a project are one of the main sources of contention between owner/contractors and subcontractors. Strict mechanics lien laws in most states allow subcontractors and suppliers to place liens against property on which they have performed work and not been compensated. Such liens take precedence and must be resolved before you can obtain permanent financing. You can control your budget and avoid aggravating and potentially costly disagreements with subs by insisting that all changes and their costs be recorded using a Change Order Form. Often, subcontractors have Change Order forms. Make sure such forms include a description of the change work that must be done and the cost involved. The order should also mention the original agreement on which the changes are based.

Obtain **Lien Waivers** when releasing final payment to a subcontractor or supplier. The Lien Waiver is a written acknowledgement from the sub that they have received all payments due them. This prevents a sub from deciding several months after receiving their final check that some of the work they did was actually extra. A good time to obtain a signed Lien Waiver is when you deliver the final check. Meet the sub at the jobsite and ask them to sign; hand them the check when they hand you the signed form. *Never mail a final check with a blank Lien Waiver enclosed.*

The **Roof Factor Table** is used to calculate the surface area of pitched roofs. This figure is used for calculating required quantities of shingles or sheathing. Even if your log home package includes these items, it's a good idea to calculate quantities for yourself to insure that they are correct.

The **Abbreviations and Formulas** page is useful for translating units of measurement from one form to another. The table includes units you are most likely to encounter.

Finally, if you plan to perform any actual labor on your home or simply want to better understand the terminology and procedures used by your subs, use the **Resources** list for helpful publications and other resources.

Daily Site Report

Project Name: _____ Date: _____

Site Manager: _____ Initials: _____

Weather: ❑ Fair ❑ Overcast ❑ Rain ❑ Snow
     Temperature: ❑ <32 ❑ 32-50 ❑ 50-80 ❑ >80
     Wind: ❑ Still ❑ Light ❑ High
     Remarks:_____

Workers on site:

_____Foreman/Crew Leader	_____ Bricklayers	_____ Masons
_____Foundation	_____ Concr. finish	_____ Excavator
_____Plumbers	_____ Electricians	_____ HVAC
_____Framers	_____ Trim Carpenters	_____ Roofers
_____Insulators	_____ Drywallers	_____ Painters
_____Cabinet Installers	_____ Floor Finishers	_____ Other
_____Ceramic Tile	_____ Floor Coverings	_____ Other

Remarks: _____

_____

_____

Equipment on Job: _____

_____

_____

Work Completed: _____

_____

_____

Work in Progress: _____

_____

_____

Equipment/Material Needs: _____

_____

_____

Visitors/Conversations/Problems Noted: _____

_____

_____

Conditions of Site: ❑ Satisfactory ❑ Unsatisfactory
Explain: _____

_____

Subcontractor/Supplier Record

_____ Item*   License # _____

Company Name _____

Address _____

_____

City, State, Zip _____   _____   _____

Phone   (_____) _____

Fax   (_____) _____

Website _____

Contact Name _____

Phone _____ Ext. _____

E-mail _____

References

Name _____   Phone _____

Address _____

City _____   State _____   Zip _____

Name _____   Phone _____

Address _____

City _____   State _____   Zip _____

Name _____   Phone _____

Address _____

City _____   State _____   Zip _____

☐ References Checked   ☐ License   ☐ Bank   ☐ Certificate of Insurance

* Item refers to subcontractor/supplier tyle (plumbing, windows, lumber, etc.)

Change Order

Change Order # _____   Date: _____

Project/Owner's Name: _____

This Change Order results from (check all that apply)

☐ Owner/Contractor Request   ☐ Subcontractor Request   ☐ Design Error

All Change Orders must be approved by Owner/Contractor prior to start of any work covered by this agreement.

Description of Changes Requested:

_____
_____
_____
_____
_____
_____

Adjustments in Subcontract Sum:

a. Original subcontract sum _____
b. Changes by previously approved Change Orders _____
c. Subcontract Sum prior to this Change Order _____
d. Amount of this Change Order _____
e. New Subcontract Sum _____

_____   _____   _____
Print Name of Subcontractor   Signature   Date

_____   _____   _____
Print Name of Owner/Contractor   Signature   Date

Waiver of Lien

(Date) _____, _____, 20____

In consideration of value received, I/We, _____
(subcontractor or supplier name), do hereby waive and release any and all liens or
right to a lien under the Statutes of _____(State) Mechanics Lien Law on
all accounts including but not limited to labor, materials and services furnished to
the date noted on this waiver on the building(s) and premises owned by
_____ (property owner name).
situated in _____County, State of _____ and described
as _____
_____
_____
_____

In signing this agreement, I further acknowledge that I am owner or employee of
said subcontractor and am authorized to execute this agreement.

Signed _____   _____
           (Subcontractor's Name)   Date

_____
           (Subcontractor's Title)

Roof Factor Table

Use the Roof Factor Table to determine the surface area of roofs to be covered by shingles, sheathing, etc. using the flat roof drawing dimensions. Multiply the flat area covered by the roof including overhangs by the appropriate pitch factor to determine the actual roof area.

Rise	Pitch Factor	Rise	Pitch Factor
3	1.031	8	1.202
3-1/2	1.042	8-1/2	1.225
4	1.054	9	1.250
4/1/2	1.068	9-1/2	1.275
5	1.083	10	1.302
5-1/2	1.100	10-1/2	1.329
6	1.118	11	1.357
6-1/2	1.137	11-1/2	1.385
7	1.158	12	1.414
7-1/2	1.179		

Example: A rectangular house has outside dimensions of 40 feet x 24 feet. The roof overhangs 2 feet on all sides and the roof pitch is 9:12, what is the surface area of the roof that will need to be covered by shingles?

1. First calculate the flat area covered by the roof:

   44   x   28   =   1,232 SF

2. Then multiply flat area by the pitch factor:

   1,232   x   1.250   =   1,540 SF

   Use 1,540 to calculate roof materials

Abbreviations and Formulas

ABBREVIATIONS

Inches	IN
Linear Feet	Lin. Ft. or LF
Square Feet	SQ. FT. or SF
Square Yards	SQ. YDS. Or SY
Squares (used for shingles)	SQS. Or SQ
Cubic Feet	CF
Board Feet	BF

CONVERSIONS

Square Foot (SF)	144 square inches
Square Yard (SY)	9 square feet
1 Square (used for roof area)	100 square feet
1 Cubic Yard	27 cubic feet
1 acre	43,560 square feet
1 square mile	640 acres

BASIC FORMULAS

Squares, rectangles or parallelograms	Length x Width or Height
Area of a Triangle	1/2 Base x Height
Area of a Circle	$3.1416 \times Radius^2$ OR $Diameter^2 \times 0.7854$
Circumference of a Circle	Diameter x 3.1416
Volume of a Cube	Length x Width x Height
Volume of a Column	$3.1416 \times Radius^2 \times Height$ OR $Diameter^2 \times 0.7854 \times Height$

Resources

I have found the resources listed here, pertaining to both log homes and general construction topics, especially useful in planning and building log homes. There are numerous good resources available on construction, general contracting and design. The selection on log homes is more limited. If you have access to the Internet, I suggest searching one of the large online bookstores or visit my website at www.easyloghome.com.

Periodicals

Country's Best Log Homes
Homestead Communications Corporation
11305 Sunset Hills
Reston, VA 20190
(800) 219-1187

Log Home Design Ideas
McMillen Communications
P.O. Box 500
Missouri City, TX 77459-9917
(800) 310-7047

Log Homes Illustrated
Goodman Media Group
419 Park Avenue South
New York, NY 10016
(212) 542-7100

Log Home Living
Homebuyer Publications
4200-T Lafayette Center Drive
Chantilly, VA 20151
(800) 826-3893

Log and Timber Style
Wiesner Publishing LLC
7009 S. Potomac St.
Englewood, CO 80112
(888) 397-7600

Resources (continued)

Fine Homebuilding
Fine Woodworking
The Taunton Press
63 S. Main St.
P.O. Box 5506
Newtown, CT 06470-5506
(800) 888-8286

Journal of Light Construction
Hanley-Wood LLC
186 Allen brook Lane
Williston, VT 05495
(800) 375-5981

Books

Log Homes Made Easy
by Jim Cooper
ISBN: 0811728471
Publisher: Stackpole Books, 2nd edition , 2000
Paperback, 272 pages

Complete Guide to Building Log Homes
by Monte Burch
ISBN: 0806974869
Publisher: Sterling Publications, 1990
Paperback, 406 pages

The Very Efficient Carpenter: Basic Framing for Residential
Construction
by Larry Haun
ISBN: 156158049X
Publisher: The Taunton Press, 1993
Spiralbound, 224 pages

Working Alone: Tips & Techniques for Solo Building
by John Carroll
ISBN: 1561582867
Publisher: The Taunton Press, 1999
Hardcover, 160 pages

Resources (continued)

Wells and Septic Systems
By Max and Charlotte Alth
ISBN: 0830621369
Publisher: Tab Books, 2nd edition 1991
Paperback, 262 pages

Building and Restoring the Hewn Log House
by Charles McRaven
ISBN: 155870325X
Publisher: Betterway Publications, 2nd edition 1994
Paperback, 162 pages

Roof Framing
By Marshall Gross
ISBN: 091046040X
Publisher: Craftsman Book Co, 1989
Paperback, 475 pages

The Not So Big House
by Sarah Susanka
ISBN: 1561581305
Publisher: Taunton Press, 1998
Hardcover - 199 pages

Creating the Not So Big House
by Sarah Susanka
ISBN: 1561583774
Publisher: Taunton Press, 2000
Hardcover - 264 pages

Log Home Shows and Exhibitions

Log Home Living and Timber Frame Home Shows and Seminars
4200-T Lafayette Center Drive
Chantilly, VA 20151
(800) 826-3893

Log Home and Timber Frame Expos
#10-3435Westsyde Road
Kamloops, B.C.
Canada V2B 71H
(888) 564-3976

Resources (continued)

Financing Institutions Specializing in Log Homes

Waterfield Mortgage Log Home and Systems-Built Housing
(888) 932-5647 (WFC-LOGS)

M&T Mortgage Corporation
Attn: System Built
2270 Erin Court
P.O. Box 7628
Lancaster, PA 17604-7628
(800) 539-1160

Websites

Log Home Plans Online
www.loghomeplansonline.com

Log Homes Made Easy Online
www.easyloghome.com

Log Home Project Planner

by **Jim Cooper**
author of **Log Homes Made Easy**

A workbook for planning and managing your log home construction project

Contains:

✓ Bid Request Forms
✓ Detailed Cost Estimating Forms
✓ Construction Calendar Forms
✓ Miscellaneous forms such as:
  •Lien Waiver
  •Daily Site Visit Report
  •Subcontractor/Supplier Record Form

The Log Home Project Planner is designed for managing the construction process regardless of the type of log home.

The *Log HomeProject Planner* is a system of over 220 pages of forms and worksheets arranged to follow the normal construction sequence. Instructions are included and forms and worksheets are designed to be reproduced.

Log Homes Made Easy
——2nd Edition——

My husband is finishing up being our "general contractor" for our log home. He found Jim Cooper's book on log homes invaluable for all of the advice. Good Luck!
...Beth

What's Inside:
- ✓ **Myths and Realities**
- ✓ **Acquiring Land**
- ✓ **Financing**
- ✓ **Comparing Log Home Companies**
- ✓ **Finding and Managing Subcontractors**
- ✓ **The Construction Process**
- ✓ **Maintenance**

Order Form

Please send me the following . . .

_____ copies of <u>Log Homes Made Easy</u> at $16.95/copy $_____

_____ copies of <u>Log Home Project Planner</u> at $24.95/copy $_____

Shipping/Handling (add $4 for first book + $2 for each additional) $_____

Missouri Residents add 6.225% Sales Tax $_____

Total $_____

Fax Orders: (636) 587-7998 Send this form.
Telephone Orders: (888) 511-1378
email orders: orders@easyloghome.com
Postal Orders: Log Home Books, PO Box 169,
Eureka, MO 63051 (636) 587-7999

Please send more FREE information on:
❏ Workshops/Seminars   ❏ Consulting

Send to (PleasePrint):

name _____

address _____

city _____ state ____ zip ____

e-mail address _____

METHOD OF PAYMENT

__ check or money order
(made out to Log Home Books)

__ Visa/MC   ___ Discover   ___ AMEX

_____
card number

_____ _____
exp. date Cardholder Name

I understand that I may return any item for a full refund—for any reason, no questions asked.

Log Home Project Planner

by **Jim Cooper**
author of **Log Homes Made Easy**

A workbook for planning and managing your log home construction project

Contains:

✓ Bid Request Forms

✓ Detailed Cost Estimating Forms

✓ Construction Calendar Forms

✓ Miscellaneous forms such as:
- •Lien Waiver
- •Daily Site Visit Report
- •Subcontractor/Supplier Record Form

The *Log HomeProject Planner* is a system of over 220 pages of forms and worksheets arranged to follow the normal construction sequence. Instructions are included and forms and worksheets are designed to be reproduced.

The Log Home Project Planner is designed for managing the construction process regardless of the type of log home.

Order Form

Please send me the following ...

_____ copies of <u>Log Homes Made Easy</u> at $16.95/copy $_____

_____ copies of <u>Log Home Project Planner</u> at $24.95/copy $_____

Shipping/Handling (add $4 for first book + $2 for each additional) $_____

Missouri Residents add 6.225% Sales Tax $_____

Total $_____

Fax Orders: (636) 587-7998 Send this form.
Telephone Orders: (888) 511-1378
email orders: orders@easyloghome.com
Postal Orders: Log Home Books, PO Box 169,
        Eureka, MO 63051 (636) 587-7999

Send to (PleasePrint):

_____
name

_____
address

_____
city   state   zip

_____
e-mail address

Please send more FREE information on:
❑ Workshops/Seminars   ❑ Consulting

METHOD OF PAYMENT

__ check or money order
     (made out to Log Home Books)

__ Visa/MC   ___ Discover   ___AMEX

_____
card number

_____
exp. date   Cardholder Name

I understand that I may return any item for a full refund—for any reason, no questions asked.

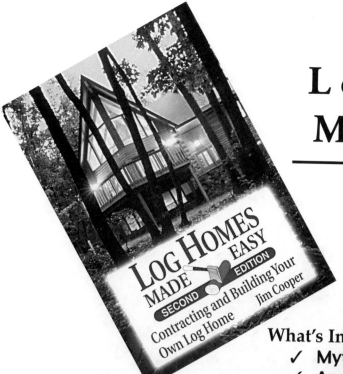

Revised in 2000!

Log Homes Made Easy
—2nd Edition—

My husband is finishing up being our "general contractor" for our log home. He found Jim Cooper's book on log homes invaluable for all of the advice. Good Luck!
                                                    ...Beth

What's Inside:
✓ **Myths and Realities**
✓ **Acquiring Land**
✓ **Financing**
✓ **Comparing Log Home Companies**
✓ **Finding and Managing Subcontractors**
✓ **The Construction Process**
✓ **Maintenance**

Order Form

Please send me the following ...

_____ copies of <u>Log Homes Made Easy</u> at $16.95/copy $_____
_____ copies of <u>Log Home Project Planner</u> at $24.95/copy $_____
Shipping/Handling (add $4 for first book + $2 for each additional) $_____
Missouri Residents add 6.225% Sales Tax $_____
Total $_____

Fax Orders: (636) 587-7998 Send this form.
Telephone Orders: (888) 511-1378
email orders: orders@easyloghome.com
Postal Orders: Log Home Books, PO Box 169,
            Eureka, MO 63051 (636) 587-7999

Please send more FREE information on:
❑ Workshops/Seminars   ❑ Consulting

METHOD OF PAYMENT

__ check or money order
        (made out to Log Home Books)

__ Visa/MC   __ Discover   __ AMEX

_____
card number

_____ _____
exp. date Cardholder Name

Send to (PleasePrint):

_____
name

_____
address

_____
city   state   zip

_____
e-mail address

I understand that I may return any item for a full refund—for any reason, no questions asked.